T0354678

MEDICAL ENCOUNTERS

MEDICAL ENCOUNTERS

TRUE STORIES OF PATIENTS – MEMOIRS OF A PHYSICIAN

SURINDER JINDAL

PARTRIDGE
A Penguin Random House Company

To order additional copies of this book, contact
Partridge India
000 800 10062 62
orders.india@partridgepublishing.com

www.partridgepublishing.com/india

CONTENTS

DEDICATION

The book is dedicated to the memory of my parents who guided me to enter the medical profession, my teachers who trained me, my students and innumerable patients who continue to teach me medicine.

ACKNOWLEDGEMENTS

I greatly value the contribution made by Robin Gupta, a former senior civil administrator and distinguished author who spent a lot of time in going through the manuscript and writing the foreword.

I wish to acknowledge the support extended by Dr. Dheeraj Gupta who was prematurely snatched away by God. He was a great colleague and a friend who stood with me through thick and thin. I also recognize the contributions of my colleagues in the department, including the late Dr. S.K. Malik who preceded me as the Head of the Department, Dr. D. Behera who took over the reins after I left, Dr. Ashutosh Aggarwal, Dr. Ritesh Agarwal, Dr. Navneet Singh and several others who were my partners in the management of many of the patients mentioned in the book.

I like to record my sincere thanks to Dr. Meenu Singh, the Jindal family including Jagdish, Krishan, Ramesh, Vijay, Raj, Dinesh and Dr. Kittu Garg for going through the manuscript. My family particularly Umesh, Aditya, Sheetal, Manishi and Rajneesh deserve credit for their encouragement and for useful suggestions and additions to the book.

Finally, I am thankful to Partridge India, Publications which provided the opportunity for the publication of the book. Without the support of their team at, it might not have seen the light of the day.

FOREWORD

Dr S K Jindal, a brilliant internationally recognized physician decorated with a lifetime award by the Indian society for chest diseases, has writer's ink flowing in his veins. After a celebrated career of practicing and teaching medicine at the Post Graduate Institute, Chandigarh and covering himself with numerous honours in India and from across the globe, he has written an enriching and beautifully crafted collage of short stories based on fifty years of clinical encounters with people from different walks of life.

These finely detailed memoirs, born of an eclectic and contemplative mind that has keenly observed the human imbroglio are the account of a sensitive and compassionate doctor who has made it his life's mission to alleviate human suffering through the treatment and cure of sickness and disease, often beyond the call of duty. In the process Dr Jindal, a natural raconteur, has incisively commented upon prevailing mores and superstition at different levels of society. The pen portraits reflected in this fascinating book encompass the lives of Governors, Prime Ministers, highly placed officials, Judges, army men, police officers, newly married couple, precocious teen agers, drug addicted foreigners, wealthy men and farm labourers in its mind boggling gamut, makes for a compelling story of life and the living process.

The author employs a direct style of writing and his command over Queen's English in these times of abbreviated idioms, is music to the ears. The short stories that are essentially about the aspiration and concerns of a patient's life as indeed the attending doctor's dilemma resonate with an undercurrent of philosophical sadness dwelling on man's purposes on earth during an all too brief existence. And all along, the author displays an unusual depth of understanding of classical civilizations and religious epics that have guided the destiny of mankind.

For the author, the persona of patients who came to him for treatment was of as great interest as the disease with which they came and the author tried throughout to preserve the individual identity of each patient rather than consign them to a bed number. The book describes the author's interactions with his patients when they were ill and in need of sharing the story of their life.

'Medical Encounters' is not a critical analysis of the fall of man; with quiet understated humour the author tries to understand rather than to judge. In this fascinating memoir Dr Jindal escorts the reader from rural Punjab to the princely state of Malerkotla where he spent his childhood and early youth to Le Corbusier's city of Chandigarh where he worked for four decades and made his home.

As one progresses through the book the reader gains an exceptional degree of information about the rhythm and pattern of medical establishments as well as the psyche of patients and medical men in changing circumstance. The stories in this book are of universal, abiding interest with a lingering vista of the future.

Ever in command Dr. Jindal like a grand puppeteer, with the wave of his magical wand, infuses life into the dying. The reminiscences recorded by him with felicity are difficult to put down. 'Medical Encounters' is a judicious selection of his best writing. I have greatly enjoyed reading the book and have no doubt, so will connoisseurs of good writing.

Robin Gupta

New Delhi 31st July 2015

PROLOGUE

'Medical Encounters' chronicles the stories of patients seen by me during a long span of clinical practice of about half a century including the first few years as a medical student. I have included only a few of those examples to keep it short. Each patient had a different story to tell even when the medical diagnosis was similar to that of others. For my own interest, I had always attempted to dig into the issues beyond the routine medical prescription and management. For me, the persona of the patient was as important as the disease with which he came. This was helpful to handle a problem more effectively, even if only with a partial success.

In a busy clinical practice, one tends to deal with diagnoses and treatments but ignores the person in the background. Disease, than the patient, is the primary target for the doctor. The identity of an individual patient, after being labelled as a 'case' or a 'bed-number', is lost in the busy and complex world of medicine. It is therefore important to bring that character to the forefront.

Each character in a story in this book has a real person in the background. To maintain confidentiality of an individual, I have changed the names, places and a few other characteristics of patients described in different stories. However, it would have been meaningless to use a pseudonym for Jayaprakash Narayan, the quintessential leader who led the national movement during the 1970s. His story is a part of documented history. I have also retained the original names of my teachers who find mention in some of the stories.

The book describes my interactions with patients when they were ill. The descriptions therefore do not necessarily represent the usual personalities of those individuals. My purpose was to describe as I saw them during sickness rather than to study their personality traits. For example, the political prisoners kept in the hospital during the Emergency period suffered from additional problems which were partly medical and partly political. They would have perhaps behaved differently if they had been free. Similarly, the people in senior positions of authority and power were not as weak or helpless in discharging their responsibilities as assessed by me during brief periods of time. I have tried to remain focused on my personal interaction with them. I might have interjected some bias of my interpretation of what transpired between me and my patients. I could not avoid that bias. I shall like to be excused for my narrow assessment of understanding.

While working at a premier Medical Institute (Postgraduate Institute of Medical Education and Research, Chandigarh), I had the opportunity to treat patients belonging to different socio-economic and educational backgrounds. I used to almost daily encounter a large number of ordinary people – shopkeepers, office employees, students, teachers, farmers and labourers who came with different illnesses. Not infrequently however, I also had to face people placed in highly important positions of power.

It was a different experience with each individual. However, one thing was common between the ordinary people and the privileged classes– they all suffered from the pain of an illness.

The different stories span a long period of over four decades. Medical technology has made tremendous advances during this period. A lot of what I read and saw during my student days may not be even relevant now. Moreover, there have been differences in attitudes and behaviour of patients as well as doctors over different time periods – before and after the era of internet. Patients these days are more aware, empowered and demanding. On the other hand, doctors have come under pressure, are stressed and overstretched while working. All these factors have also affected a doctor's handling of patients. There have been several changes in prescription patterns over these years.

I remember the stories of Bhag Singh and Naseebo of the early 1970s who could be successfully managed with preliminary technology of that time, even though Jeet Singh could not survive. On the other hand, we have strange stories from the modern 21st century. It was difficult to believe the tale of Inderjeet who lived a stigmatized life, an internet-misguided Bobby and a secretive Mr. Singh. Superstition and gullibility persists even in this era of knowledge-explosion. It would sometimes seem that much has remained unchanged in-spite of the drastic transformation of medical technology.

For me, each encounter with a patient has been a lesson in human behaviour as much as an experience of disease-management. Each patient along with his family presents a complex interplay of emotions, ambitions, expectations and frustrations while fighting with an illness. I find each story as a mixture of pain and pleasure, hope and despair, as well as of success and failure. There is a bit of sarcasm in some of these encounters without the intention of any reflection on the personality of an individual. Though I have tended to avoid the medical jargon as much as I could, I might not have been successful all the times. In case of confusion, the reader may refer to the glossary given as an appendix at the end.

S. K. Jindal

1.

CHILDHOOD ADVENTURES

I can vividly recall the images of some of my treatment sessions for a few injuries in early childhood. The treatment was provided by half-baked, small-town *practitioners* who used to work with a few tablets, lotions and syringes without ever going through the portals of medical training. I can also see my father and sometimes a few other members of my larger family supporting me to go through those treatments. Some of those scenes seem similar to those depicted in the paintings of surgical operations or amputations being performed by priests or surgeons seen in the books of history of medicine.

To sit in front of a doctor over half a century earlier, was a ghastly task especially for a young child. A doctor was always a fearful person while a surgeon was the cruellest of men. Thank God, it is no more so. Sitting in my chamber in a position of authority, which is though somewhat diminished from that in the past, I tend to compare a patient in front of me to what I was in my childhood. I have two physical souvenirs on my body reminiscent of my childhood adventures– the scar of an old wound on my calf and restriction in rotational movement of one of my forearms. It is quite likely that the early life experiences were responsible for my parents encouraging me to join medicine.

My family belonged to Dhuri, a small town in Punjab where I did my schooling. However, it was in a nearby town Malerkotla, where I had my early encounters with 'medical doctors'. Malerkotla was an interesting place with a glorious history. It was founded by Sheikh Sadruddin-i-Jahan from Afghanistan, subsequently ruled by his *Sherwani* descendants. At the time of Indian freedom from British rule, Malerkotla was an independent State governed by a Muslim *Nawab* held in high esteem. It had a dominant Muslim population. The State was blessed by revered 10th Sikh Guru Gobind Singh ji in recognition of the humanitarian support of Sher Mohammed Khan, Nawab of Malerkotla during the early 18th century when the two young sahibzadas of the Guru were ordered to be tortured and buried in a brick wall by the then Governor of Sirhind.

In 1947, the town had remained free of the mindless violence and the frenzy of riotous crowds seen elsewhere in the state. At that time, a large number of people from surroundings areas, mostly Muslims, flocked to the town when riots broke out in the region. Tragically though, the Hindus and the Sikhs moved out fearing counter violence. Malerkotla was one of the first States which acceded to the Union of India.

We had moved to Malerkotla when my father, who was a *qanoongo* and later a *tehsildar* in the revenue department of the government of Punjab, was transferred to the town. We rented a large spacious house which was built in an old colonial style. The place was available at a bargain since there was hardly a family agreeable to live at the place. It had been earlier inhabited by a wealthy Muslim relation of the *Nawab* who had moved to Pakistan. Ours was the only Hindu family in an exclusive Muslim neighbour-hood. Most of our relatives were highly sceptical of the move and had advised my father against shifting to that place. But my father was rather resolute. His belief in his religion, faith in the Guru's blessings and confidence in the *Nawab* helped him to face resistance of all the family. We never regretted the decision and enjoyed an excellent relationship with our neighbours.

Besides the aura of his official position, my father possessed a powerful and fearless personality. Most importantly, he was immune to rumours which were rather common in those days. Suspicions flew all around. People in the area were generally illiterate, poor as well as credulous in beliefs. They were fearful of demons and gods alike. They looked up to my father for guidance and troubleshooting. In due course of time, we got conditioned to the neighbours who started sharing their festivals such as *Eid* with us. We were strict vegetarians in our habits. Hesitatingly, they would offer us uncooked rice or *sevians* which my mother would cook in our own kitchen. We greatly relished the food and enjoyed that relationship.

The local community was riddled with superstitions and illiteracy. Every day, we were told stories of ghosts who were moving around in the house. People would describe their shapes in great detail making it hard to doubt the narratives. The ghosts were huge in size and shadow-less, had unkempt hair with long fingers and nails. They had blood-red eyes, Dracula like teeth and feet directed backwards. We would intently listen to the tales with rapt attention. Someone would tell the stories of *spirits* of people who had been butchered and buried in the lawns of that house some centuries earlier. Others would even spot a dancing demon on the *neem* tree under which we calmly slept throughout the night in the summer. Almost every ailment was attributed to one or the other evil force which had taken possession of the body. Remedies used were even more curious, and frequently monstrous. I faintly recall seeing more than one girl being treated with devious means such as beating with a broom and the use of red chillies in the eyes to 'force out' the spirits. The *ozhas* had a good running business in the town.

While on a long air-travel, I recently had a chance to flick through some stories about ghosts in a book, 'A Twist of the Knife' by Peter James. I developed goose bumps on my skin after reading his first-hand experience of ghosts in a haunted house. I realized that the Malerkotla house we had lived in a few decades earlier had an identical history. Fortunately, we ourselves did not encounter any moving spirit of the dead. I now wonder if things would have been different had we believed in the existence of the paranormal. I am thankful to God that we were blissfully unaware.

The neighbours appreciated our courage and conviction but were truly fearful of potential damage to us by the evil ghosts. My mother, a simple and hard working woman with traditional values would often accept what others said to her. However, each time my mother was warned to be wary in the name of God, my father would not listen.

Sometimes in the late 1950s, I had climbed a tree in the front-lawn of my house. Finding it difficult to climb down, I shouted for help. My mother was busy with her work inside the house. Without realizing the problem, she sternly replied – "Come down yourself in the same fashion you had climbed up". That was a great challenge to my acrobatic capabilities. Angry at the rebuff, I decided to climb down on my own. As luck would have it, I slipped, struck a branch and ended up with a big, lacerated wound on my calf. I was taken to a local general practitioner who was famous as *'Refugee-doctor'*. A victim of the partition during Indian independence, he had moved to this town from West Pakistan. He, without a degree of his own, was known to have worked with some doctor in Lahore. He bandaged the wound after applying some highly irritating and painful lotions. The same painful process was repeated everyday till I recovered over the next few weeks. It was the tender care provided by my mother which helped me to carry on. Both my mother and I had learnt a lesson each. We promised each other to be careful in future.

My promise to my mother was rather short-lived. Within perhaps a year, I broke my right forearm after a fall while playing. I was given some kind of a splint dressing by the same *'Refugee doctor'*. He was quite gentle with his approach. Before the fracture could completely heal, I fell again. That was considered as more serious requiring consultation with a known *'bone expert'* in the nearby town. Unlike modern orthopedic doctors, the concerned *expert* was a field worker who earned his living doing small time jobs. He was known as a *dhadia* who used to weigh cereals in the market. A strong and muscular man, he was popular in the region because of his penchant for special massage therapy for relief of pains in bones and joints. He would fully justify his muscular build when giving massage. I can never forget his treatment sessions. He tried to correct my fracture with the use of his great power. It caused me excruciating pain each time he would manipulate my arm. Somehow, it healed after a period of several weeks. Later during my medical career, I came to know that both the bones of my forearm had joined together, technically called as cross-union. Fortunately, it did not cause any problems with my work but for mild restriction in rotation of the forearm.

Having experienced the *bone-expert*, I shudder at the work of *surgeons* of the medieval era in Europe on patients in the absence of the luxury of anesthesia. The surgical procedures were often done by barbers who besides cutting the hair and doing minor surgical procedures, would even amputate limbs and extract the teeth. The patient was forcibly held by several men throughout the procedure to let the surgeon do his work. The b*arbers-surgeons* were also in great demand in the Christian monasteries to tonsure the hair of monks and do regular blood-letting as per the traditions of that time. There were frequent conflicts between doctors and barbers. To me it always seemed that a barber-surgeon in the middle ages would have done a better job with the limbs than the *bone-expert* of my home-town in the 1950s.

Superstitions were not restricted to the community in Malerkotla. But for the ghosts and dancing spirits, the situation was no better in Dhuri, the city we moved to when my father got his new posting. Dhuri was also the place where most of my uncles and their families lived and where I shared a larger part of my teenage life. The whole city was scared when a team of health workers engaged in vaccination program against small pox, visited schools to inoculate children. Students ran away from classes to avoid injections. Parents of children were concerned at the '*devilish' objectives of English experimentation on poor Indian children*. "Why should Nehru accept the evil designs of the British? India is a free country now." People tended to criticize most such health programs. My mother was quite protective of me and my younger brother when we came back home for fear of forced vaccination. My father got the news in his office. He sent a message to my uncle to take us back to school. All the school-going boys and girls in the family were duly vaccinated.

All poxes were considered a curse bestowed by the *mother goddess* for unknown sins committed by the victims. Small pox was the bigger and chicken pox the smaller sin contrived in the names of the *mother goddess*. All kinds of offerings were made and worship done to appease the goddess. If the patient got better, the goddess was supposed to be pleased. Deterioration on the other hand, implied her anger. Fortunately, the vaccination program was continued in spite of the obstacles posed by opponents. In due course of time, small pox was one of the few diseases which could be eradicated from India.

As time passed, awareness improved and people became conscious of modern medical practices. But the vagaries of past had hardly gone. Almost over three decades after the vaccination program, somebody whispered somewhere to some-one that the marble-statues of *gods* drank milk. The news spread like a wild-fire throughout the region. No-body was bothered about the source of the news. People made the lord's statues drink milk in temples and vouched for the veracity of the claim. This set me pondering on why only a few miracles of God looked wonderful? We see the enormity of miracles each moment of our lives without batting an eyelid. A tree growing out from a tiny seed, the suns and the stars shining in the sky, the mountains and the seas are all miracles which man has seen for millions of years. Is not the very basic fact of birth, growth and death equally mind teasing? It is perhaps the oddity which makes people mull over facts. In the case of God's statues it took weeks for the euphoria to die down. Soon the miracle vanished into thin air.

A lot has changed since I first faced the refugee doctor in his clinic. In spite of the pain and anguish of the treatments, I cannot deny the relief provided by the two '*doctors*' whom I faced in my early childhood. They had played their roles with honesty and conviction and for that I pay my homage to them. One cannot judge the past with current standards or modern parameters. But one thing is there to see and believe. It would be erroneous to think that the times have changed. Modernity has not guaranteed an insurance against misadventures in medicine. We continue to find out-dated practices all around.

The incidence of the broken bones revisited us recently after more than half a century. A maid who worked for us at home fractured her wrist when she slipped on the stairs. We tried our best to get her treated by an orthopedic surgeon. The treatment required the wrist to be immobilized in a Plaster-of-Paris cast. Her husband opted for treatment from a *bone-expert of dhadia fame.* The woman had little choice in the matter.

Our journey to reason and logic in medicine has been rather slow.

2.

DISSECTION HALL

After the rigmarole of pre-medical education, I got admission to the Government Medical College at Patiala where I started with my M.B.B.S. course. The very first day at the college was an experience to remember. The introductory lecture by a senior professor from the Department of Anatomy was more of a warning than a welcome. After almost an hour of torture, we were directed to move to the dissection hall. We were required to spend most of the days in the dissection hall for the first one and a half year. Physiology, another subject included in the syllabus for the First semester would start much later.

The first sight of the dissection hall was mind blowing, almost a shocking experience. The wooden tables with marble-tops were laid out with naked human bodies (or their severed limbs), ready for dissection. In spite of warnings given earlier by senior students, I was not really prepared for the actual scene. It was scary and a bit tragic but far removed from the pictures of mummified bodies or zombies which one often sees in horror movies. The shrivelled, motionless cadavers lent a feeling of grief and serenity to the scene. That vivid moment is deeply etched on my mind as if to constantly remind of the inevitable end to life. After about fifty years from that day, I now know that life comprises of a never-ending but moving cycle.

The College was the second medical school established in resurgent Punjab after the tragic partition of 1947. Named after Maharaja Rajendra Singh of the erstwhile Patiala State, it was started in the early 1950s with a large faculty formed by a number of senior professors trained in England. Some of them had moved from the erstwhile King Edward Medical College, Lahore. The Medical College was famous for the distinguished faculty as well as being particularly recognized for some of the work on *fluorosis*.

Admission to a medical degree was a great event to celebrate at home not only for me but for the entire family. To some extent, it pleased the entire neighbour-hood at Dhuri. I suddenly assumed the label of a doctor even before entering the gates of a medical college. Some of my relatives and other acquaintances would seriously ask for remedies for their problems. I could perhaps have easily settled in 'medical practice' like my old friend, the *refugee doctor* or the *dhadia*. But destiny had meant it otherwise and I opted for the harder course to go through the tribulations of a medical career.

Life in the medical college was altogether a different proposition than studies in a degree college. My heart was full of happiness, but I was greatly anxious and somewhat scared. I had been already cautioned by friends about a tough life, full of long hours of hard-work and sleepless nights. The immediate concern however, was the fear of ragging by senior students, and nagging by teachers. Dissection Hall was one of the target places for ragging.

A sharp and pungent smell greeted me the moment I entered the dissection-hall, less than a hundred meters away from my hostel-room. I soon learnt that the smell belonged to formalin vapours which were ubiquitous in those surroundings. A bit of formalin in the environment became a part of my life quite soon. Formalin was extensively used for preservation of cadavers and body-organs in the Anatomy and Pathology museums. It was also used for mopping of hospital floors as well as for fumigation of operation theatres and intensive care units. The use of more sophisticated and less irritating materials has partly replaced the traditional hospital-smell in most of the modern hospitals. Not infrequently, some of the public hospitals in India provide a *deja-vu* of the sixties and seventies.

The initial shock and sadness in the dissection hall were temporary as a group of senior students sneaked in and started to rag the new entrants. They were obviously conditioned to the surroundings in the Hall. In spite of the repeated warnings by the college administration, the ragging practice had continued. The torture period used to last for a few weeks and end with a welcome party on a friendly note. It was not entirely uncommon for ugly incidents to occur occasionally, sometimes with disastrous consequences. The practice exists till date in spite of restrictions, sometime inviting punishments and even the wrath of judicial courts.

Peace was restored with entry of Prof. Thapar who was a popular teacher in the subject. He was known for his dissection skills as well as personal humility. He was particularly sensitive about the handling of cadavers. Due to a shortage of cadavers, groups of students were allotted various body parts to dissect. My group of six students, including three girls, was given the upper limb to dissect and study the details over a period of 6 weeks. The other limbs, the trunk and the head of the body belonged to five other groups. Space around the table was quite precious with about 25-30 students sharing a cadaver. We all had to work in rotation. It was only after about 2 weeks when the limbs could be separated from the main body and taken to different tables that adequate space became available for everyone to sit and work with comfort.

'Dissection is an art' – was the first lesson we learnt on the table. It was amazing to know that human-dissection had been performed since the third century BC with varying periods of legalization or proscription. Dissection in the prehistoric periods was perhaps performed to search for "differences" between the living and the dead. There is mention of cases of human dissection in ancient texts of several civilizations including 'Susrutasamhita', and 'Sutrasthana' of Ayurvedic literature. During the Christian era, the Catholic Church had itself ordered an autopsy on conjoined twins to check if they shared a soul. Based on the finding of two hearts, it was decided that there were two separate souls – the heart was always believed to be an abode for the soul in the past.

Pioneer anatomists like Vesalius and Leonardo da Vinci, used human-dissection for their excellent anatomical descriptions made during the medieval period. Some of the original drawings of human structure drawn by Leonardo da Vinci hold great scientific value for their details even in the present era. Vesalius in the 16th Century conducted a public dissection of the body of an executed felon which he stole after the execution. He re-assembled the bones and preserved the skeleton. It is now famous as the Basel Skeleton, displayed at the Museum of the University of Basel in Switzerland. William Harvey, the man who first described circulation of blood in the human body in the 18th century, is known to have dissected the bodies of his father and sister.

The demand for human bodies for dissection considerably increased at the newly opened medical colleges and universities in the 19th century. Therefore, trade in the human skeleton became quite remunerative. In earlier centuries, a large number of executions were carried out by the State. Therefore, bodies for dissection were available with ease. But by the 18th and early 19th centuries, the number of executions significantly diminished. As a result, *"body snatching"* became a de facto profession. There were several instances of thefts of bodies from graveyards. The matter progressed so far that the 'body snatchers' found it easier to kill people and sell their bodies rather than dig up graves. Things came to head when two infamous cases involving multiple murders came into the public eye.

Burke and Hare in the early 19th century used to smother and kill their victims to sell to Doctor Robert Knox for his anatomy lectures. The crime came to be known as *burking* after the name of William Burke. Soon thereafter, there were other suspicious murders for which Bishop, May and Williams were tried and sentenced to death. They had tried to sell a body at King's College School of Anatomy after refusal of Guy's Hospital. Herbert Mayo, the professor of anatomy who informed the police suspected foul play since the body of the dead boy was fresh and appeared unburied. The authorities were compelled to enact suitable laws to regulate the procurement of cadavers for dissection in medical schools.

In spite of a strong likelihood of human dissection being performed by ancient Indian physicians and surgeons, the practice was considered a great taboo in modern India. Indian students especially from the higher caste Hindu families did not opt for Western medicine for fear of touching dead bodies. The taboo to dissect human bodies was broken by Pundit Madhusudan Gupta who got his training in medicine from the United Kingdom. He was a Sanskrit scholar as well as an Ayurvedic physician. He along with his students performed the first human dissection on 28th October 1836 in Calcutta Medical College. He was given a fifty round firing salute by British authorities from Calcutta Fort William. This event can also be construed as the beginning of Western medical education in India.

Human cadavers for dissection are difficult to procure these days. Of late, a number of people opt to donate their bodies for dissection after death. However, body donation alone is not likely to meet the enormous need for a vastly expanded number of medical students. The practice of manual dissection is being replaced by virtual dissection and computerized simulation modelling. This has obviated the need for human bodies to some extent. For people like me, the old method of dissection remains the gold standard.

During our training, we followed Cunningham's manual which was the standard text book guide in conducting dissection. The instructions were given in inquisitive detail and one would find things exactly as written in the book. There was nothing more satisfying than to discover the structures described in the book as one proceeded layer by layer into the human body. It is a wonder how the human mind adapts to different situations. As the time went on, we all became casual in our handling of body parts until strongly rebuked one day by another brilliant teacher, Dr Makhni. He would not tolerate any careless placement of or disrespect to a piece of bone or dried soft tissues. He always kept on reminding us that the parts belonged to humans like us who must be respected for their contributions to our training. 'In death they live and teach' was a lesson we remembered forever. The sanctity of human life, even after death, must never be violated.

Dr. Inderjit Dewan a reputed and the senior-most anatomist of the region, was our external examiner in the final anatomy examinations. He had a reputation as a tough but fair examiner. I was asked by him to dissect out the *left internal mammary artery*. This vessel by virtue of being commonly used for *coronary artery bye-pass grafting*, is quite familiar these days to the doctors and the lay alike. With his long forceps for which he was quite well known, he held out a thin branch of the artery and asked me for identification. *"Pericardio-phrenic branch of the internal mammary artery"*, I replied rather nervously. He did not ask any other question and abruptly left the table, obviously pleased. Dr. Thapar informed me later that the branch was relatively rare to find on routine dissection by a student. I therefore earned his pleasure and merit in results. I had an excellent relationship afterward with Dr. Dewan at the Postgraduate Institute in Chandigarh where I later served. Dr. Dewan had joined the place as the Head of the Anatomy and Forensic Medicine Departments after his retirement from regular service as the Principal of the Medical College, Rohtak.

The images and impressions of the dissection hall were almost permanent. Years later, when I chanced upon a human skeleton in a classroom of the medicine department in Chandigarh, my mind went instantly back by almost a decade while memories of the dissection hall flashed in front of my eyes. I for one did not forget the lessons taught by Dr. Thapar, Dr. Makhni and the like. A lifeless human body is reminder of a limited life span. It also reflects the continuity and eternity of life. I have always felt that the sensitivities and sensibilities in handling patients as human beings are actually learnt in the dissection hall. Those who can handle the dead with respect, also handle the living with concern and affection. I recapitulate below the lesson I learnt from the skeleton at that time.

Lesson of a Skeleton

I escaped the journey to the Heavens in not being offered
to the sacred Ganges.
It was not in my fate to travel to Eternity
by being buried in the lap of mother earth – unseen and
unknown.
It was left unto me to stand here in the glass-box,
to face you and remind you of your existence.
I am here to teach you the lesson of immortality, and not
the death.
How can I explain to you that within this hard bony frame
existed an individual who breathed and lived as you do.
But you are the 'present' and I, the 'past'.
Both you and I are the same inside.
Throw away the mask, and you shall recognize yourself.
You will know the real meanings of a wonderful life worth
living.
You will realize the futility of hiding 'skeletons in the cup-board'.
Be bold and open your cupboard.
The hidden skeletons will come out and merge in you.
The skeleton is a part of your existence.

3.

PATIENT WITH SCALDED PALMS

After successful completion of about one and a half years of Anatomy, Physiology and Biochemistry, I got posted in the hospital to learn about clinical methods. The very first *case* which I presented for a clinical-bedside demonstration became a history for me to remember. I was allotted a patient in the Skin Out-patient Clinic to prepare and present to the class. He was a middle aged individual in his forties who appeared to be apparently healthy. About a year earlier, the patient had noticed redness of the palms of both hands. Logically, he attributed the redness to his habit of holding hot cups of tea between his palms. I was also familiar with that common practice amongst the working class. Hot tea was served in locally prepared, disposable clay mugs with no handles to hold. Tea and milk continue to be served in similar cups in several parts of India especially at the railway stations and road-side tea-stalls. He did not have pain or any other symptom, therefore did not bother for treatment. After about a few months, the redness changed to black discoloration along with scaling of skin. At that stage, he decided to seek medical opinion.

I took a good long history as per standard format described in Hutchinson's Manual of clinical methods which was followed in the College. The skin on the palms was blackened, thickened and encrusted and had peeled off at places. It almost amounted to scalding of palms. The overall general physical and systemic examinations were normal. I organized my thoughts and suitably prepared my discussion for the class in the afternoon. Bed-side case presentation was the standard practice of clinical teaching. To date, it has remained a tradition for over a century in most parts of India.

I was greatly puzzled as to how could a person hold a burning hot mug which could scald the hands. I was somewhat annoyed at the gross negligence of the patient for being indiscreet. 'How could he damage himself in such an ugly fashion', was all I could think? Was he drunk or drugged when that happened? I discussed the case with a few other fellow-students who were equally confused. We all agreed that the teacher wanted to demonstrate the appearances of scalded skin to us, the novice. We patiently waited for the after-noon class. I did not bother to think beyond what was apparent.

My presentation went fairly well. Prof. Handa who took the class was pleased with my description of the lesions, but that was all I could boast of. I was not prepared for the volley of questions which followed.

"Why do you think that he scalded himself like this?" asked Dr. Handa.

"He was rather foolish to be careless, or may possibly have been drunk" I replied.

The answer was enough to replace the perpetual and infectious smile of Dr. Handa with an angry frown. He was obviously not happy at my flippant response.

"Did you examine the sensations of his hands?" I kept silent. He continued: "One does not drink hot tea after a heavy bout of alcohol. A drunkard may accidentally get burns from hot water or tea but will not be injured symmetrically in this fashion".

I had obviously made a fool of myself. Using an ordinary paper pin and a wisp of cotton, he demonstrated there and then that there was a total loss of pain and other sensations. The patient had hurt himself from over-heated mugs since he never sensed the heat. It was the loss of sensations including the pain, which was responsible for repeatedly prolonged contact with the hot cups, without the realization of risks. We were further told that the damage to the nerves in that patient could be attributed to *leprosy*, a dreaded disease. In all fairness, the learned teacher had never expected me to make a diagnosis of *leprosy* but I should have demonstrated, or at least thought of loss of sensations as a cause of symmetrical burns over palms.

The diagnosis of *leprosy* came like a bolt from the blue. I had to swallow my pride. Till that time, *leprosy* in my mind was confined to the roadside beggars sitting in front of temples, or to people one saw in colonies and slums. It was not at all believable that I would see such a case in an apparently healthy, working individual. There was hardly any doubt that the individual had scalded his palm from close contact with hot cups of tea. We were further told that involvement of nerves in *leprosy* would frequently result in loss of the toes of the feet due to persistent injuries from pressure, trauma, heat and cold. It was also responsible for de-pigmented patches over the body with loss of touch and pain. The diagnosis of our patient was soon confirmed on slit-smear examination of skin, and treatment prescribed. I did appreciate the importance of going into the depth and to think about the "Why" for every clinical problem.

Leprosy as a *sinful disease* had continued to haunt society all over the world. That people suffering from *leprosy* were shunned and abused in the past is a known historical fact. Those patients considered as highly contagious and cursed, were condemned to live in isolated colonies and not allowed to enter the cities. The disease has a history of over 4000 years dating back to the ancient civilizations of China, Egypt and India. It possibly appeared in Europe after the army of Alexander the Great returned from its invasion of Asia. In pre-biblical India, the 'Laws of Manu' prohibited contact with leprosy and punished those who married into their families. 'Leper colonies' were separately established. *Leprosy* patients were sometimes burnt alive in some of the medieval societies.

Of umpteen stories on the subject, the 1959 block buster Hollywood movie *Ben-Hur* beautifully depicted the agony of Miriam and Tirzah, mother and sister of *Ben Hur* who contacted the disease in prison and were condemned to live in the '*Valley of the Lepers*'. They were shown to get cured of leprosy while witnessing the crucifixion of Jesus. '*Adventures of the Blanched Soldier*' by Arthur Conan Doyle was another story reminiscent of the curse of *leprosy* even in the early 20th century. The brave soldier who returned to England from the Boer war was completely hidden from the world by his family and locked in his house as he was suspected to suffer from leprosy. It is a different matter that the master detective, Sherlock Holmes with the help of an expert physician diagnosed him to suffer from 'pseudo leprosy' or "*ichthyosis*". The man was happily rehabilitated back into normal life.

I learnt of several other causes of loss of sensations and surface burns in the following months and years. A number of medical causes of skin-scalding due to persistent heat exposure were quite interesting. Women sitting in front of domestic furnaces for heating in winters frequently developed skin pigmentation due to burns, called *'erythema ab igne'*. Kashmiris carrying *'Kangri'* – an earthen pot containing burning coal, under their robes to keep themselves warm are known to develop abdominal discoloration, burns and skin cancers. Similarly, the fishermen along the coast of Orissa and Andhra Pradesh, who are in the habit of smoking *'chhutta'* – a 'reverse form' of smoking tobacco with the burning end of the *'chhuta'* kept inside their mouth, develop leukoplakia of mouth, as well as the oral cancers. None of those conditions however, would produce deep skin burns as one would see in conditions where the surface sensations are lost, for example in leprosy or other causes of neuropathic disorders.

Gerhard Hansen of Norway had first found the mycobacteria – a type of micro-organism that caused *leprosy*. The great discovery had brought great hopes of cure for the patients. Subsequent discovery of effective drugs to kill the causative organisms had helped to control the disease, the world over. In place of *'Chaulmoogras oil'* which had been used for centuries for treatment of leprosy, the drug therapy has significantly improved. The multi-drug chemotherapy which has now become available is much better in achieving a radical cure with a potential of elimination of the disease from the world. The day is not far when medical students will no longer need to include *leprosy* in the differential diagnosis of scalded palms. Even though pockets of *leprosy* remain in some parts of India, the disease is no more considered either as a sin or as untreatable.

I never had the chance to know what happened to my first patient in the following years. But he suddenly returned one day to help me do better for one of my Post-graduation examination in Medicine after several years. A young teen was shown to me as a *short case* for quick examination. A number of students had made wrong diagnoses. The boy had a small patch of skin discoloration on his back which was noticed by his mother. I made a careful examination and made a mental list of causes of de-pigmentation. I thought of *leprosy* at the top of the list but was scared to make that diagnosis in a well-placed, school going youth. Suddenly, my friend with scalded palms flashed back in my mind. He reminded me of the lesson I learnt that day. I immediately supplemented my examination with tests for touch and pain. The boy had no sensation over the patch. I did not think twice but almost blurted out the diagnosis to the grand examiners - 'Once burnt, twice shy!'

4.

LABOUR WARD

Pregnancy constitutes a highly significant part of a woman's life of which labour is the critical culmination. Both the events form a popular theme for authors and artists who tend to portray the subject from different points of view. Thousands of versions can often be seen in the Maternity wards of hospitals. I had heard a number of stories associated with labour in my own hospital. It was during my posting in the labour ward when I had the chance to personally witness the melodrama associated with delivery. It was then that I realized the difference between what is truly seen from what one hears from others.

As a final year student, I was posted in the maternity ward for a week. That was an essential curricular requirement to be completed before one could appear for the Final Examinations. The first night of my duty had all the ingredients of a Hindi feature film. After a day full of boredom, I had my dinner and slept in a dormitory meant for the medical students. There was a hard knock on my doors after midnight. The caller asked me to immediately rush to the Labour Room to assist the duty house surgeon. The nurse in the Labour Room informed that a woman named

Naseebo, who was admitted only a few hours earlier had progressed to *"near full dilatation and ripening of cervix"* – the signs of impending delivery. The on-call registrar (senior resident) was already on her way. I did not wish to miss the chance to include the patient in my log-book of deliveries. I was supposed to have attended at least ten deliveries (or so).

There was a total dominance of women doctors. In North India, only an occasional male-doctor used to opt for the specialty of Obstetrics and Gynecology in spite of some of the eminent names in the subject being men even at that time. The trend in several Southern and Eastern states had been different where males accounted for a large number of obstetricians. I could notice a kind of female-chauvinism in the department. We, the undergraduate students were practically non-existent for the regular staff members of the Labour Room as well as for the post-graduate residents in Obstetrics and Gynecology. We were treated as unimportant, dismissed as non-entities.

The fate of male postgraduate residents was the worst. They were considered rather burdensome for the specialty. They formed the butt of many jokes. "How can they become good obstetricians? Only the bearer knows where the shoe pinches". Another girl would comment: "I wish that the boys get an equal opportunity to become pregnant". Nonetheless, the boys carried on with their pursuits. Some of them also managed to find good life partners from amongst the girl residents!

No one could match the zeal with which those girls worked in the ward. They remained on their toes throughout the days and nights. Some of the woman doctors were married with young children. One could not fail to appreciate their endurance as they practiced hard in addition to looking after their families. Hats off to a female obstetrician who carries on with that labour-intensive specialty as well as patiently goes through her own pregnancy and labour!

Naseebo was a *primi-gravida* who was crying like hell with labour pains. To me, she appeared in great distress needing immediate help. But others in the labour-room were not convinced. They remained unmoved in spite of her loud calls for anesthesia. No one even bat an eye-lid at her shouts. When I tried to argue for some treatment for her pains, I was rebuked. "It seems that you are more distressed than her. You perhaps need an injection of a tranquilizer", commented the nurse-in-charge. That was enough to keep me quiet for the next hour.

The house-surgeon Dr. Khosla, only about two year senior to me, took the charge. She was quite deft in handling such situations. She took a few minutes to wash her hands and forearms before moving to the side of the patient. She started cajoling, encouraged her to push more and more. Her sermons were also interposed with challenges and rebukes.

"Come on! Show the strength of a brave villager."

"Which community do you belong to?"

"*Jat Sikh*? Do not insult your community."

"Don't they serve you good food at your home?"

"Push more! Yes! A little more! Well done. Go on."

The next scene was an anti-climax. The patient suddenly evacuated her bowels on the table. This was somewhat nauseating for a sophomore. Dr. Khosla folded the sheet containing the stools, disposed it off in the waste-bin in a workman like manner. I could hardly utter a single word.

I was given the duty to regularly monitor the fetal heart-rate and patient's blood pressure. Some degree of fetal distress had meanwhile developed which was a cause of worry for Dr. Khosla. She was anxiously waiting for the registrar to arrive and decide if a *cesarean section* should be urgently done. Suddenly, the nurse shouted that the head was clearly visible. The baby was due to come out soon. Immediately, an incision called *episiotomy* was made and delivery aided with the application of forceps. Fortunately, the *Cesarian section* was not required. The baby was grasped by the nurse in her hands and wrapped in a sheet. As soon as it cried everyone else in the room relaxed. I meekly joined the laughter of people in the room. The *placenta* also got soon expelled.

Peace was soon restored. Immediately after the pangs were over, the mother spoke: "Is it a boy or a girl?" That was the first and the only question which the mother had asked.

"See this is a healthy and handsome boy" told the nurse with a smile.

Naseebo slipped into sleep without waiting for any further explanation. She had got what she wanted, including the *license* to prove her dominance in the family. Birth of a son has been a symbol of mother's pride in a traditional Indian family. That was particularly so for a village woman like Naseebo.

The *episiotomy* was stitched and a dressing applied. There was now a calm atmosphere broken by the cries of the baby. He too was shifted to the Nursery. I was greatly impressed by all the action scenes. Soon Dr. Khosla moved on for the next venture to attend upon the next labouring patient. I was greatly exhausted and sleepy but sheepishly followed her footsteps. I needed to complete my log-book in that very week.

Next morning, Naseebo was shifted to the Maternity ward which presented a rather chaotic scene. Unlike expectant mothers in the labour-room with tension and anxiety writ large on their faces, women in the Maternity ward were quite relaxed. The mothers of new born babies recovering from their labour wore the proud look of a winner after a gruesome battle. They continuously chatted without any inhibition. They had their own shares of woes with multiple new symptoms which were not given adequate attention. The duty-doctors mostly considered their complaints as inconsequential and largely purposive. I was told by an intern: "It is the time for these mothers to seek greater attention of their 'in-laws'. At a subconscious level, they fabricate symptoms to get rewards from husbands. Do not pay too much attention to what they say on the rounds."

The ward could be singled out as a place of happiness and content in the hospital. One could spot old ladies sitting around the beds congratulating their daughters or daughters-in-law. One could also notice women who consoled their wards for the pain and soreness with poetic justification: "Nothing comes cheaply – certainly not a child. You have got a *diamond*. Only he (*rather she*) who would search for pearls must dive below". Naseebo was similarly praised by her family. I wonder if the expressions would be as intense if the child were a girl.

Interestingly, the Maternity ward remains the only place in a hospital where a patient gets an added value for her admission than in any other ward of the hospital. In a medical or a surgical ward, one can at best regain the same health status as before the occurrence of illness. There are positive gains in obstetrics wards. For students, the rounds in Maternity ward provided pleasure far removed from the terrifying scenes of the labour-ward. Surprisingly, the shrieks of labouring women had little effect on the doctors and nurses in the room. It was the quietness which seemed to bother them more.

It was primarily in the labour room that I learnt the importance of a thorough hand-wash for prevention of infections. I was narrated the story how mortality following delivery was controlled in the 19th century. Ignaz Semmelweis in Vienna and Oliver Wendell Holmes in Boston had observed a high incidence of *puerperal fever* which frequently led to an unacceptable rate of deaths of women following child birth. It was observed that medical residents attended upon deliveries in the labour rooms immediately after conducting autopsies without washing their hands. It was hypothesized that "*cadaverous particles*" were carried by the medical doctors and students on their hands straight from the autopsy room and transmitted to the labouring women.

Semmelweis' recommended that hands should be scrubbed in a chlorinated lime solution after leaving the autopsy room before attending to a patient. The implementation of that measure led to a dramatic fall in the mortality rate. It is an entirely different matter that it took several decades before the nature of the *'cadaverous particles'* i.e. the micro-organisms, came to be known and the simple measure of hand-washing was widely adopted.

There was nothing extra-ordinary in the case of Naseebo from what I saw in the next few days. I had similar experiences with other women whom I witnessed in the labour-room. I completed my work assignment within a week. After my MBBS, I had opted for post-graduation in General Medicine. Being a physician, I never had a chance to conduct a delivery. I can only claim to have looked after my pregnant wife when none else from the family was there in the United States. Even that care was never up to her satisfaction level. Unlike most of the American husbands, I had chickened out of the room to witness the delivery first hand as was the practice in that country. Indian husbands were too shy and meek to be present during a tough task!

For the rest of my life, I did not attend to deliveries but had to listen to stories of pregnancy or of infertility at my home on most days. My wife and later on my daughter and daughter-in-law chose Obstetrics and Gynecology for their professional careers. That helped me to understand the problems related to pregnancy and labour in a very different perspective. It was then that I learnt that the pain of not bearing a child was several times more than the labour-pains. A woman enormously enjoys the onset and progress of labour-pains, but for the terminal intensity which becomes humanly unbearable. That is why doctors employed different strategies like those in the sixties and seventies which sometimes appeared to be rude. The wider availability of "painless delivery" methods and an early recourse to *Cesarian Section* in modern days has significantly altered the overall scene of delivery.

I also had multiple opportunities to provide consultations for medical problems complicating pregnancy and/or labour. Diagnosis and management of routine medical conditions during pregnancy is always tricky. There are special considerations with drugs as well as the tests in view of the potential risks to the baby besides the mother herself. One is always guided by the enormous medical information which is available on these issues. On the other hand, it has been more difficult to advise girls and boys suffering from chronic medical problems, and more so their families on issues related to marriage, pregnancy and labour. I had to however wait for several years before I faced those issues in my professional life.

The labour-ward duty not only made me eligible to prepare for the Final MBBS examinations, but also enabled me to do duty without being distracted by shouts and shrieks. More importantly, nothing was smelly any more in the future! On the other hand, a visit to the Maternity ward used to provide immediate rewards. Despite being students, we were frequently offered sweets by happy and grateful mothers. Living in hostels away from our homes, we would always grab the opportunity. Ever since, there has been no shortage of sweets, with an obstetrician wife at home!

5.

BHAG SINGH

I had moved on to begin my internship after the Final term examination. Internship involved rotational training in different specialties for varying periods for the total duration of a year. This was a mandatory step in order to qualify for the MBBS degree. I had several different experiences during internship; some of the most disturbing patients which I saw belonged to the surgical specialties. The large ulcerated tumours sometimes infested with maggots, the gangrenous limbs and the chronic wounds oozing with blood were ghastly to look upon. Early intervention and treatment would have checked the progress of these lesions but was not possible in most cases. Most of those patients were poor while ignorance and lack of availability of treatments added to the woes.

Rotation in the surgical wards was generally depressing. Broadly, the ward presented a scene one sees following a disaster. I have no intention to disturb my readers with description of surgical problems. I always gave a great degree of credit to surgeons who could handle the problems during the day and still sleep at night with ease. It took quite some time before I got conditioned to those types of patients.

Some of those *cases* were worse than the grotesque pictures of advanced problems shown in the Bailey and Love's text book of surgery which we read. Thankfully, most of those types have now become rare, even though there is no dearth of unfortunate victims with surgical deficits and disabilities. People continue to be maimed by acts of terrorism, violence, and traffic accidents in addition to the disasters like an earth-quake or a tsunami.

Even in the surgery wards, there were a few bright sparkles here and there. Bhag Singh was one such example who defied the otherwise poignant scene of the ward. Bhag Singh was a brave soldier who had weathered over twenty monsoons in the jungles. He used to tell his stories with great pride and never tired of repeating the detailed descriptions of his excursions. He had several encounters with enemy forces when he served in the British Army before Indian Independence. He boasted of facing volleys of bullets of the Japanese Army during the Second World War. Even more dangerous were the attacks of mosquitoes in the jungles of North East India and Burma. "There were greater numbers of deaths due to mosquito-bites than from the actual war. We had to face '*king size*' mosquitoes which 'equalled or exceeded the size of large cockroaches'. Doctor Sahib, the fight with insects in those forests was most demoralizing." With good luck on his side, he had succeeded in his war with the Japanese as well as the mosquitoes. He had survived all onslaughts, retired from Army with honours.

I have always found that a soldier takes greater pride in his service than any other type of worker. He serves with a greater purpose than merely to earn a salary for a living. He does not hesitate to risk his life for that purpose. He likes to enjoy his achievements with exaggerated descriptions of strange events and experiences. Bhag Singh was no different. But the poor fellow was now down with cancer of the urinary bladder. I had learnt of his problem when I faced him first time on a night-duty.

I was called to attend upon him well past midnight by the Staff Nurse-in-charge. He had not passed urine for over 24 hours and was writhing with pain. The true valour had fled from his face. He was in a deplorable state in sharp contrast to the image which he projected in his day-time stories. I was shocked to see his plaintive look.

"Why did'nt you tell during the evening rounds that you did not pass urine?" I asked.

"I did not have pain at that time" he replied.

"Did you have your normal intake of food? How much water did you consume today?"

"Oh, yes. Everything has been quite well until now".

Possibly, he had intentionally evaded the question. He had lied about everything being normal until then. Perhaps he did not consider it important. Perhaps it would have hurt his pride to admit of a symptom of old age. More likely, he was ashamed to talk of the urinary problem with a youngster like me. I was too young for him to accept as a competent person to handle his problem.

I patiently examined his abdomen. His bladder was full, rather over-distended due to urinary retention. He would not tolerate even a gentle palpation. I tried to reassure him, gave an analgesic shot and prepared for urinary catheterization. I checked his case-file to look for the notes by the resident-in-charge. Not much was mentioned but for a few scribbled sentences on his history of present illness. Surgery residents have always been poor to document details of patient history. One had to talk to the concerned resident to get any sense of the problem.

It was not easy to get things going. Organizing even a minor procedure at night was quite a nightmare in the over-crowded ward. The ward was overflowing with almost three times the number of patients than the number of available beds. Around two thirds of patients had to be content with '*floor-beds*'. There was hardly any space to move about and carry the procedure-trolley to the bedside. Bhag Singh had managed a regular bed to lie upon. But for a very few serious or otherwise prioritized patients, each one had to wait his turn for a regular bed. Not infrequently, each patient used to bring one or the other recommendation for an early bed allotment. Only a lucky patient could hope to get a bed within the first 2 to 3 days of admission. The turnover was rather fast and one could also hope for an early discharge from the *floor-bed*.

It was somewhat difficult to pass the catheter into the bladder. I did not possess the expertise of an experienced resident. Independently, I had undertaken only two or three catheterizations before that night. Moreover, he was struggling throughout the procedure. I succeeded after application of a lot of anesthetic jelly, a repeat injection of an analgesic and a good amount of talking. But the relief following catheterization was dramatic. Around two liters of urine were quickly drained. Everything seemed to be so simple but for the underlying disease from which he suffered. That was not the cause for the worry at that moment. He thanked me profusely for my expertise which I knew was rather meager. His wife joined him in showering praise. I wish I could take similar pride for my work as he had done.

Even after over forty years of that incidence, the situation in a large number of government hospitals is no better today than in those days. The public sector continues to suffer in view of the large crowds and ever increasing treatment-costs. Standard treatments are frequently sub-optimal. There have been tremendous improvements and up gradation of services. A lot of disposable materials have replaced the old rubber catheters and glass syringes which were washed and repeatedly used. It is a different matter that the disposable materials have added to rather than solving the problems.

Catheterization on that day helped me earn my prize next morning. Bhag Singh narrated an exaggerated version of the events of last night. He profusely showered praise on me at the Professor's rounds in the morning with all the medical staff of the Unit. My friends were smiling each with a tongue in cheek. But my stock had considerably risen thereafter in the surgery department for that night-time labour.

I came to know more of his illness in the next few days of my duties in the surgical ward. His stories were unstoppable, often unbelievable. Several of his descriptions could well be listed in the Guinness Book of world records. Besides the *king-size* mosquitoes, he claimed to have seen an elephant-sized tiger and confronted a rhino which subsisted by eating jungle-deer. He had once fallen in a *mile-deep* trough and escaped unscathed. Neither me, nor others would believe in all what he said. But every-one listened to him with great interest. I can now claim to have visited the North Eastern States of India as well as the neighbour-hood

Myanmar (earlier Burma) for professional meetings or conferences. Every visit would make me remember my old friend even though I could never corroborate his experiences either on my own or from the local populace. It was obvious that he used to apply a big multiplication factor to all his measurements.

He was operated for his tumour after a few days. As the tumour was far advanced it could not be removed in total. Surgery was followed by radiation treatment which was largely palliative in nature. When discharged, he had a fairly content look and hoped to live long for another ten years at his farm in his village. He did not show any concern for the nature of disease or about its future progression. He tended to be will-fully ignorant. His only worry was to somehow avoid urinary catheterization in future.

I had prepared his papers for discharge from the hospital. He got a bit emotional, invited me to visit his village. I never had the pleasure of seeing him again.

6.

EMERGENCY WARD

The Emergency Ward of the Postgraduate Medical Institute at Chandigarh was the first place where I was directly responsible for patients. I had joined the Residency program in the department of Medicine, after about five and a half year of my undergraduate course. The very first posting in the Emergency department had a dampening effect on my enthusiasm. It seemed as if an electric shock treatment was necessary to administer before one would start with clinical duties. However, after the initial jolts, I did get conditioned to the highly labile environment of the Institute which fluctuated between extremes of hot and cold temperaments. In the long run, it became quite enthralling; I spent the next over forty years of my professional career at the Institute. In due course of time, I had the pleasure to share in the Golden Jubilee of the Institute in 2013 before my superannuation. In fact, I had the honour to co-chair the Celebrations Committee.

The Postgraduate Medical Institute at Chandigarh, popularly known as 'PGI' was and is one of the most sought-after places for postgraduate medical education and training in India. The Institute continues to occupy a position of eminence in the country till date. Inadvertently, it also served as a step-ladder for medical graduates who dreamed to move abroad. The pattern of education imparted at the Institute, at par with the West, enabled a large number of students to successfully compete for Residency programs in the United States. However, I had never wished to migrate to foreign lands. Admission to the PGI- program was a dream come true.

As luck would have done it, I got my first rotation of Residency in the Emergency. Truthfully, it was considered to be the hardest posting which involved a tight work-schedule of over 12-hours at a stretch each day. Moreover, the duties were boring, tough and repetitive in totally unfamiliar surroundings. I had hardly any interesting work to do but to fill out requisition-forms, and draw blood from patients who invariably grumbled. Because of repeated blood sampling which was often done, we used to call ourselves as '*blood suckers*'. Scribbling entries in patients' files was the only light work to do. I even thought of going back to my medical school but was dissuaded from making that mistake by Dr. S. S. Jolly, a Professor of Medicine from Patiala who had developed a soft corner for me.

I felt like a caged prisoner moving like a dummy on orders of the medical Registrar rather than a doctor. Even the people with whom I worked were different, sometimes indifferent. The Reddys and Raos, or Mukherjees and Banerjees got added to the list of Singhs, Sharmas and Guptas of the region. Occasionally, I would even find a white man speaking in an accent which I could hardly understand. Some of the names of colleagues were difficult even to comprehend. Till then, in the absence of television and internet, I used to read about them in the newspapers; now, I was mixed with them. My world previously was limited to a very narrow region. It had suddenly expanded. I felt lost in its length and width. I soon realized that the PGI presented a picture of cosmopolitan India. It gave me the first chance of direct contact with *'other people'* – an opportunity which I loved for the rest of my life.

The feelings were no different for students from the rest of India. Most of them had moved away from their home-towns. They found it even harder than me to adjust. A colleague of mine from Andhra told me of his great discomfort when he arrived on a cold December night. The temperature at the Chandigarh Railway Station was low and cruel. He started shivering the moment he stepped out at the platform. He went back to the cabin and declared that he wanted to go back to Hyderabad. It was only after persuasion by others that he finally managed to come out and move to the campus. In the next few days, he got appropriate warm clothing to condition himself.

Surprisingly, some of the residents from the South remained comfortable with far less warm clothing than us. A hard-working surgeon from Madras State (now Tamil Nadu) who later became a brilliant urologist and moved to U.S.A. was never seen wearing more than half- sleeved shirts and pants with a pair of *'chappals'* without socks, even in the coldest days of winter. His prototype dress soon became the subject of humour among the entire resident population. On the other hand, the residents from Kashmir tended to cover themselves with even more layers of clothes than they would do in Kashmir. It seemed that only the *sons of the soil* from Punjab were adequately dressed.

The Emergency ward was always full of serious patients. Patients from distant places from the surrounding states preferred PGI as the first choice for treatment of all kinds of medical and surgical emergencies. It was sometimes shocking to find that people would tend to transport even a bleeding or a convulsing patient from a faraway place to the PGI, rather than taking him or her to the nearest hospital. To my horror, I realized the gravity of this problem within the first few days of my Emergency-duties. The incident also gave me strength to do away with my existing dilemmas and doubts.

I was only a few weeks into my training when a young person in the early third decade of life was brought late in the evening just as my duty was about to end for the day. He came with a history of massive bouts of vomiting of blood at home. Even in the hospital, he was almost pouring out. There was a crowd of highly anxious relatives accompanying Jeet Singh. He was pale and sweating, incoherent and delirious. His blood pressure was hardly recordable. His condition made me tense. Anxious and fearful myself, I looked to my Registrar for guidance. Before he could arrive from a neighbouring ward, I succeeded in establishing a venous line and starting saline administration. I also took the blood sample to send for cross-matching and blood requisition. By then, Dr. Mahapatra, the night-Registrar was available to take over and direct the management. He also asked the surgery-resident for his opinion and discuss with his own consultant in-charge for any additional intervention. A *Ryle's tube* was inserted through the patient's nose for cold water lavage after emptying the stomach of its blood content.

Blood aspiration created a mini-disaster in the ward. Already panicky, the relatives in the corridors were greatly alarmed. One of them finally decided to be bold and question my wisdom of siphoning the contents of the stomach.

"What is the hurry to take samples? Please do not cause any further damage. Already, he has lost a lot of blood."

"Do not worry. This blood in the stomach is like a waste, of no help."

"So what? It is the stomach from where he has bled. It is better avoidable."

I was immature in dealing with those types of situations. I could not convince them that the blood in the stomach was lost to the circulation. It was only after the explanation by Dr Mahapatra that they could be convinced. Even afterwards, the constant sight of blood being removed with the syringe did not provide for a soothing picture.

With great difficulty, we succeeded in arranging a few units of blood for transfusion. Availability of blood was generally poor, except during the days following a voluntary blood donation camp. It was quite shocking, and remains so even now that few relatives and friends agree to donate blood. It was a common joke amongst residents to ask for blood donation whenever one wished the unwelcome and over- enthusiastic well-wishers to vacate the corridors of the crowded Emergency.

Jeet Singh was transfused around 8 to 10 bottles of blood overnight. The surgeons could not find an obvious cause of bleeding, therefore decided against any surgical intervention. I could go back to my hostel only several hours after my duty was over. The scenes kept on reverberating in my mind throughout the night. I was back in the morning at 8 AM sharp. In spite of the resuscitative measures which were undertaken, Jeet Singh had passed away in the early hours of morning before I came. I learnt with great regret that the family had created a highly charged atmosphere immediately on hearing the news. The younger members of the family particularly his sister almost assaulted the night-duty doctors and nurses. They loudly accused and abused everyone as guilty for his death. The elder members of the family were unable to control the agitated sister. With great difficulty, she was removed from the scene by the hospital-security to restore peace.

I was upset at the first death which happened under my care. I did not go through the final moment of death but almost saw it happening. Seeing my sullen mood, the day- Registrar Dr. Chopra spent some time with me. We sat in the duty-room where we discussed issues over a cup of coffee. He narrated several other incidents and told me that more was yet to come. "A doctor should be emotionally detached", he advised. "How else will you manage Surjeet or Harish or Gunjeet who are likely to come in the future? Jeet Singh is gone. We must get ready for the next!" He also warned that you do not need a disaster to keep you busy. A single '*hot potato*' is enough for a night to remain on feet throughout. More than his words, his manner and humour were quite relaxing as well as reassuring.

Dr. Chopra also made some meaningful medical statements that Jeet Singh had suffered from an irreversible shock and that precious time was lost during transportation. It would have been better to treat him at a facility nearer to his place of living. "Patients unfortunately die of damage caused by lack of immediate medical assistance – and of blood at the initial sites of mishap. Foolishly, one tends to ascribe death or disability to the last documented event. What has actually preceded and precipitated the event is conveniently forgotten. It is there that the truth is hidden".

I was not sure whether medical help was unavailable at Jeet Singh's place or if his family opted for Chandigarh on its own. But the damage was done. Nonetheless, I did find solace in what I was told. Thereafter, I was better prepared to face those tough situations.

Decades later, a similar lesson was echoed by a senior police officer who had more than once dealt with incidents of mass deaths. He himself was a victim with a disfigured face after suffering from bullet-injuries during a terrorist attack. "Jindal, people including the media criticize us for our insensitivity to death when we tend to be normal. What should we do? Should we cry and look grim-faced? We do our duties in the midst of violence. How can we face the next challenge if we remain glued to the present tragedy?" I did not disagree with a single word of what he said.

What type of life lay ahead was clear to me after that night. I never looked back. After completion of my six-year residency program, I joined the Faculty of Pulmonary Medicine at the same Institution. Meanwhile, Chopra had moved to Jallandhar, an important educational hub in Punjab where he established a large hospital of his own. After a few years stint at the PGI, Mahapatra migrated to America to practice as a successful cardiologist.

7.

JP - THE QUINTESSENTIAL LEADER OF 1975

Jayaprakash Narayan, popularly known as JP, is known for his contributions to the contemporary political scene of modern India in the seventies. He is also remembered as the quintessential mass based socialist leader whose name continues to be quoted whenever there is talk of a need for change in the system of governance. He had challenged the powerful authority of the then Prime Minister, Mrs. Indira Gandhi who had ruled democratic India almost single handed since 1966 when she first assumed power after the sudden demise of Prime Minister Lal Bahadur Shastri. Following JP's revolutionary movement for a change of government, Indira Gandhi forced a *rule by decree* by imposing Internal Emergency. She resorted to several measures to curb the widely spreading resentment which included censorship of the media and suspension of civil liberties. A large number of prominent leaders of major political parties were arrested and put in jail. JP was perhaps the most important person detained during that period. Many of our current leaders owe allegiance to his political philosophy. I remember JP for entirely different reasons.

I had the honour of looking after JP as a medical officer during the days of his political internment and subsequent hospitalization at our Institute at Chandigarh. I was one of the few senior-residents, working with the team of senior doctors constituted to look after him. The team was led by the then Director of PGI, Dr. P.N. Chhuttani. JP was detained along with several other leaders when the Emergency was imposed on 26th June, 1975. He was shifted to Chandigarh on 2nd of July for medical care, where he remained "interned" for the next four months.

It was a lovely bright morning in Chandigarh when it all started. The weather was warm and moderately humid. The campus was abuzz with different kinds of rumours including that of the arrival of a *serious and important patient* who could possibly be JP. Later we came to know that JP was brought to the Guest House and transferred to the hospital, the previous night. My first encounter with the *most significant VIP* of that time was somewhat tense in the presence of gun-toting policemen. I was asked by Dr. Chhuttani to go to the ward and prepare a standard medical records-file for JP. I took it casually and walked to the Intensive Care Unit where JP was admitted. This was a newly built ward which was yet to be commissioned. At the entry to the ward, I was stopped and questioned about my identity. That was rather annoying. No one had ever dared to stop a Senior Resident especially with a white coat on in the campus. I had no other option than to prove my credentials. After a body-search, I was led to his room by a constable.

His room was equipped with a hospital bed, an easy chair, two small tables and another writing desk with a sitting chair. He also had good number of books along with writing material. He seemed to have a limited number of clothes and other personal belongings. There was an attached bathroom whose door was later replaced to suit his convenience. There was an air-cooler in his room, though he preferred to keep it off. All efforts were made to keep him comfortable.

Our first meeting was uneventful but for my own initial hiccups. JP was quite easy and comfortable to talk to. He was calm, cooperative and polite. While responding to every greeting with a smile, he did not refuse to answer a single question. My nervousness seemed obvious to him and he did not wish to make it worse. The routine physical examination also went well. I thanked him profoundly and left the room in the company of the constable. All along, the constable was standing near the doors, quietly watching and listening to the conversation.

Throughout his stay, no one was allowed to enter his room alone. Initially, the security personnel were suspicious of each and every movement of the medical team. However, in due course of time, they got adjusted to our movements. We had been instructed by our seniors to work in an uninhibited manner without bothering about the presence of the police. "Do not annoy them but work as if they do not exist". The statement was repeated every time Dr Khattri, the immediate team-leader would visit. This was easier said than done. We did not really know how to avoid the prying eyes and ears.

We all took care to spend minimum time with JP at each visit. We only talked about his health and physical condition – something which eventually became quite boring both for him and us alike. Everything kept on happening rather mechanically. There was a deep sense of frustration, and later of regret for most of us. The hospital and its medical team were charged with dereliction of duty towards him, accused of damaging his kidneys - deliberately.

JP always complied with the routine physical examination for vital signs. He only complained of episodes of palpitations now and then; his pulse was full of irregular beats due to the presence of '*premature ectopic beats*' in his heart-rhythm. He was aware of their presence for many years. Their presence remained a cause of concern for the team of physicians and cardiologists attending to him. The initial treatment for these *ectopics* proved to be more annoying and troublesome than their presence. He developed excessive sleepiness, nausea and weakness after administration of anti-ectopic medicine. That state lasted for 2 to 3 weeks after which the culprit drug was finally omitted. His condition improved but *ectopics* returned. No attempt for their management was made thereafter.

Generally speaking, his medical condition stabilized after the first few weeks. He could sleep well, occasionally with the help of a mild tranquilizer. His appetite improved and he seemed to be more cheerful. He had adjusted fairly well to his surroundings. He did develop a small boil on his forearm, which cleared with dressing and medication. His long standing diabetes had affected his immune system. The foot-prints of diabetes could also be seen in his eyes and nerves. For most of the time, his blood sugar levels were controlled with routine orally administered drugs, which he had been using for years.

Actually, JP's health had deteriorated in the pre-Emergency period, even prior to the "Battle of Patna on November 4, 1974". Minoo Masani, a long-time friend of JP had talked about his health in his book, "Is JP the answer"? He wrote: "JP suffers from a heart condition, is a diabetic and has a chronic kidney ailment. Even the stresses and strains of this major showdown could affect him adversely". Most of Masani's fears and calculations proved to be true.

JP was simple in his living, he hardly mentioned any discomfort. His personal letters and daily newspapers were delivered to him by the prison authorities, possibly after scrutiny. The Jail Superintendent had permitted short walks in the corridors of the ward at JP's request. One of us, along with a prison deputy-superintendent, used to accompany him. We used to keep a record of his vital signs, before and after the walk. On one occasion, a novice police inspector did not wish us to accompany the "prisoner" during a walk in the open ward – he considered it a 'security risk'. By then, we had learnt to deal with the police. I strongly protested his decision, argued that the ward was not an open space to pose any risk. Moreover, each one of us was sufficiently screened before one could enter the ward. This reasoning was fruitful and the subject was not mentioned ever again.

JP felt suffocated in those roofed and closely guarded premises, even though he was allowed to move around. He often expressed that he longed to see open spaces and blue skies. He wanted to hear the noises of chirping birds and wanted to move away from the monotonous hospital environments. He did not wish for the soft and cautious medical or nursing care but for the hustle and bustle of the crowd. He preferred a prison which had an open compound than a close hospital ward which resembled an isolation cell. He did express his feelings to the Director, Dr Chhuttani and others. None of us was privy to the discussions held among the higher centers of power. Soon a decision was made to shift him to the Institute Guest House, situated within the campus, on 18th September.

The stay in Guest House was more pleasant. He could walk in the open ground without the mandatory presence of medical attendants and consultants. It was more like a house detention with which he felt better adjusted. My own visits were fewer, less than once in a week. He mostly spent his time with his books. Police constables were restricted to the outside gates. Unfortunately, his fragile health deceived him soon. He had to be shifted back to the same ward towards the end of October. His condition had deteriorated. He looked apathetic and anguished, his mood had worsened. He was no longer the same person as before. He would sleep only after tranquilizers were given, had loss of appetite and constantly complained of dull abdominal pain.

The medical condition was rather worrisome but no abnormality was detected on biochemical tests which were frequently repeated. The food which was served to him was prepared as he desired, but it became harder every day to get him to eat. He felt restless and longed to go back home. Depression was also considered as a possible diagnosis but not substantiated by the psychiatrist. Permission was now available for an occasional visit of some of his close relations. Such a visit gladdened him for a couple of hours followed by the sedate and long painful hours of the day which haunted him.

His condition went further downhill in early November. A urinary sample revealed findings consistent with urinary tract infection. He was administered with appropriate antibiotics. The senior nephrologist of the Institute, Dr. K.S. Chugh was in constant attendance throughout. Our fears about worsening of his kidney function proved true in the next few days. It was apparent that very soon he would need dialysis for the recent deterioration.

The night of 11th November was a real nightmare. By that time, he was an extremely exhausted and fatigued man. The worst was expected to happen any time. I was on duty in the adjoining Emergency Ward, with another colleague sitting in JP's ward. It was a sleepless night for all the doctors attending upon him. He slept intermittently for a few hours, with the help of drugs. Fortunately, the night passed without the occurrence of any serious event. On the other hand, there was a constant exchange of telephone calls between Chandigarh and Delhi. It was a great relief for all of us to know in the morning that he was served with release orders – on parole. He was altogether a different man in the morning. He was pleased, looked cheerful and relaxed. For the first time in the past several weeks, he ate his breakfast well. His one single comment to me was satirical and unforgettable: "The Queen has finally felt mercy on me". The first demand he made was to go to Bombay, now Mumbai, where he would stay with his brother and continue further medical treatment.

He was now surrounded by his friends who had come from Delhi and elsewhere. He could talk freely. The police had suddenly vanished. There was none of the familiar faces shadowing him. We could examine him and talk to him without restrictions or inhibitions. "I do not need you people now. You can also rest and relax", he remarked. On great persuasion, he waited for five more days as a free patient for stabilization, before being moved out. He finally left on 16th November for Delhi, en route to Bombay. Dr Khattri, the cardiologist who had brought him to the PGI from the airport on 2nd July, accompanied him to Delhi to the All India Institute of Medical Sciences, where he was to stay for a few days.

When JP was wheeled out of the elevator, we were all waiting for him on the ground floor. He cheerfully bid us good-bye with folded hands and tears in his eyes. I distinctly remember his words when he left: "I wish the best for all of you. I am very thankful for the great care and affection you people gave me, in spite of my being your prisoner". I have never been able to decide what he meant to me. Was he a patient, a prisoner, a guest, or someone else? Perhaps a bit of everything! He loved freedom and fought for the same, but he himself remained a prisoner, that too in a hospital.

A rapid succession of events followed at the national level. The Emergency was lifted in March 1977 and the general elections were held. There was widespread rejection of the Congress Party. The Janata Party, which constituted a conglomerate of several opposition political Parties won the elections with the patronage and blessings of Jayaprakash Narayan. Morarji Desai took over the reign as the new Prime Minister. Raj Narain, who had defeated the former Prime Minister, Mrs. Indira Gandhi was given the charge of the Health Ministry. Soon after, there was a period of revenge and retribution. In 1978, Dr Chhuttani was replaced as the Director of the PGI, Chandigarh. An inquiry was ordered into the nature and adequacy of treatment provided to JP at Chandigarh. Dr Koshy from Kerala was appointed to look into alleged issues of negligence; he was soon replaced by the Nagappa Alva Commission.

It was a matter of great pain and anguish for all of us that we had to face a prolonged inquisition. Several damning and illogical accusations were also made in the media. We were blamed for collusion with the previous government. A delegation of senior doctors met the then Prime Minister to seek his intervention for justice. He dismissed the issue as a joke – "Do not worry. I know that you have behaved and acted professionally. Do you really expect anything substantial to come out of this inquiry?" He was also believed to have commented: "Has any political inquiry ever been meaningful?" He was said to have publically commented on one of the ministers in his cabinet that 'every circus has a joker'.

I, like many others, appeared several times before the Nagappa Alva Commission during that period when I was supposed to enter in matrimonial relationship. The repeated postponement of my engagement date due to the Inquiry was a matter of great concern for my family and future In-laws. The issue became a subject of jokes amongst my friends. Fortunately, everyone in the two families appreciated the complex problem. I did finally marry in November 1977. Meanwhile, the Institute had challenged the Commission in the High Court. The Nagappa Alva Commission could not point out any deficiency in its Report. In due course of time, the Inquiry fizzled out. The Janata Government lost the public mandate in the next general elections merely three and a half years after its historical victory. Indira Gandhi once more returned with a massive mandate.

Sidelines

Looking after JP was a privilege, as well as an ordeal for all of us. Throughout his stay, we lived under an umbrella of suspicion and paranoia. There seemed a constant invisible watch by "big brother". People were afraid of talking in open. The police occasionally demonstrated its anger with the hospital staff engaged in cleaning and dusting of the premises. The man who used to bring food was always searched and scrutinized. The members of medical and nursing staff were more privileged. The Government found it convenient to use the hospital for its political purposes though the Institute was not meant to serve as a prison. *But who could bell the cat?* No one could raise a finger at the decisions imposed from Delhi.

My brief brush with police occurred later, when I had a chance to attend upon another Emergency prisoner detained in the same ward. An envelope addressed to me by my name contained a letter meant for the detained politician. The same was intercepted by the police. It seems that the sender, whom I never knew, wanted to play a trick to deceive the police. He had imagined that I would deliver the letter after opening the envelope. I am sure that I would not have resorted to that foolish mistake. I was put under suspicion and repeatedly questioned, though politely. The issue was finally solved at the intervention of a Deputy Superintendent of Police who could not find any wrong-doing. He told me casually that "heavy letters" always aroused suspicion of Police. Meanwhile, the Police must have checked my antecedents through its own ingenious methods.

The police and the CID staff on duty in the ward included an officer of the rank of Deputy Superintendent, two inspectors, sub-inspectors, a few constables and guards. The Police Superintendent and the Jail Superintendent used to make separate visit almost every day. An interesting feature of the whole drama was the frequent occurrence of verbal clashes between the CID and the Prison staff on one or the other pretext. The people who accompanied the doctors and others inside the JP's room belonged to the Jail staff while those waiting outside the room belonged to the CID. They remained critical of each other's actions. But both the groups used to confide in the doctors and share their concerns. They generally accepted our neutrality and infallibility. We never took sides, took care to remain non-committal.

The guards at the gate used to enter the name of each and every individual who visited JP in a register maintained for that purpose. The times of entry and departure were also recorded. Ninety, out of hundred times, the names were grossly misspelt. That was particularly so in case of doctors from South India whose names were quite unfamiliar to the poorly literate staff. They would laugh away whenever we pointed to an error. "Who bothers about these records?" was the standard answer.

Our own team which was on duty round the clock included a postgraduate Senior Resident, a staff nurse, and a ward attendant. The senior consultants paid visits a number of times each day, held free discussions and mutual consultations. The team of medical consultants which visited him at one or the other time was led by the Director, Dr P.N. Chhuttani, himself a senior Internist and Gastroenterologist. Others in the team included senior cardiologists, a neurologist, an eye surgeon, a general surgeon, a dental surgeon, an ENT surgeon and general physicians. Nephrologists were called upon towards the later part of his illness, when he was found to have kidney malfunction.

Strict secrecy was observed in every matter relating to his treatment. All the requisition requests for various laboratory tests carried the simple label of *'VIP - kidney unit'*. Though no name was ever mentioned, everybody knew the VIP whose blood or urine was to be tested. Meticulous care was observed during each test, and a careful record was made in the file. Possibly, in our sub-conscious mind we were aware of the future need to record to save ourselves from litigations. Fortunately or unfortunately, we did require the help of those records within a short period of about two years.

The procedure adopted for each radiological examination was tedious, setting an extreme example of unnecessary secrecy and security for that time. Whenever JP was taken to the x-ray department, the surroundings were cordoned off by the police and the gates were shut. Since the Radiology department was located right below the Emergency Ward, the whole area used to get cut off from the Emergency Reception and the rest of the hospital. Sometimes when specialized tests were done, the isolation lasted for hours; other emergency patients had to wait and visitors stranded. That was most undesirable but little could be done to correct the situation.

The nurses chosen to attend upon JP were carefully screened. Only those who were known to be efficient and caring were selected. The group of senior residents included a woman doctor; her visit to the ward generated fear and awe amongst security staff. She was known to be brash and outspoken. She would never listen to advice from senior staff and often fight with guards who were mortally afraid of her. At the police request, she was spared of night duties, after the first few days. Her dedication and devotion to the duties however drew general appreciation. Later, she also moved to the United States.

Our relations with the police staff were mostly cordial. They all had their own tales of a sorry state of affairs to tell. Their stories were heavily laced with instances of high handedness by their superiors. The final blame always lay at the doors of one or the other politician. They shared their experiences with us which ranged from how to subjugate a common criminal to how to disperse a riotous mob.

We enjoyed each bit of the interesting conversation. One gentleman was extremely proud of his ability to earn money from the street hawkers, shopkeepers and the loafers. Another was an expert in *traffic-challans*. He could find fault with every single vehicle, if he wished. I did not believe his claim. Perhaps he was not off the mark, considering the chaos on the Indian roads, at least now a day. Shockingly, an inspector had admitted that the police would not hesitate to fabricate evidence against any hard criminal in case of *"pressure from above"* to nail a murderer. He would try for less severe punishment for such an individual in a court of law. He for one had never implicated an innocent individual for a false murder case – all other charges were considered as fair, as and when necessary.

Most of such meetings would end with requests for our medical opinion. Everyone had a long list of bodily complaints. They found it quite convenient to have consultations for their distant relatives and friends, without having any real idea of their illnesses. They would often request for supply of *'drug samples'* and *'tonics'* from us which were supposed to be provided free by the pharmaceutical companies. We all were accustomed to such off-site consultations. I believe that many of those opinions were only meant to initiate or maintain a dialogue.

After Thoughts

Whenever I recall that period, I become quite nostalgic. In spite of the tension, I enjoyed every moment attending upon JP. Whosoever knew me used to deeply probe to know the details of his condition. All sorts of rumours were afloat in the city. People used to talk about the secret visits by top political leaders and ministers including Mrs. Indira Gandhi to win him over. *"He snubbed Dr Karan Singh the Health Minister, who came last night and proposed a compromise. He has offered JP a senior position in the Government if he withdraws the movement. But JP refused even to talk to Indira Gandhi on the phone".* It was a common belief amongst many that JP had already passed away and only a 'dummy JP' was being kept in the hospital to avoid a back lash.

We knew that most of what was talked about him was false. But rumours had a nasty way of spreading. Nothing was ever mentioned in the press which was closely censored. Therefore, the Institute could not issue a statement to refute such claims. Today, I cannot vouch for telephone calls but surely know that no senior minister from the Centre had ever bothered to pay a visit, and that he was alive but living as an isolated man amongst a large number of *dummies* in a crucl VIP ward.

I remember a few incidents which symbolized his continued interest in national and international events. He used to get hurt at newspapers' reports of floods and famine. He often felt angry at the political news of *'all is well'* in the newspapers. "There is fire underneath. The volcano will soon erupt", he remarked once during a visit of one of our senior professors. He was very sad on the Indian Independence Day on August 15 when he read about the assassination of Bang-bandhu, Sheikh Mujibur Rehman, the president of Bangladesh. Sheikh Rehman along with his family was executed in a military coup in Dhaka within a few years of formation of Bangladesh. JP was upset that India could not prevent the tragedy after ensuring the Bang-bandhu's victory in 1971. Only Sheikh Hasina, the daughter of Mujibur Rehman, who was away to Germany had survived. A couple of decades later, she was elected as the Prime Minister of Bangladesh.

Surprisingly, JP's collection lacked books on politics. He used to study the Ramayana and the Gita, almost regularly, which he might have remembered by heart. Occasionally, he would be seen reading fiction such as the 'Perry Mason' series by Erle Stanley Gardner or the detective thrillers of James Hadley Chase. "Light reading is sometimes helpful to kill the time", he would often say. Other books in his possession included 'The Constitution of India', 'Autobiography of Bertrand Russell' and Tolstoy. I never saw him reading books on economics although there were a few in his cupboard. He was a regular reader of the journal, 'The Radical Humanist', formerly 'Independent India', founded by M.N. Roy.

Books were his good friends but he could not communicate with them. They only 'spoke' but did not listen. JP had spent all his life in public glare, speaking and talking to people. He was full of grief, suffered from mental strain with pent-up anger against the system. His life resembled Kustner's in 'Darkness at Noon'. He once said to me in a very sad tone: "I shall finish, if I remain like this". Another day, while walking down in the corridor, he suddenly stopped and, cited the words of a famous Urdu poet with a sigh: *"Subah hoti hai, sham hoti hoi. Zindagi yon hi tamaam hoti hai…"* (The morning and the evening come and go; the life ends in a similar fashion).

JP was alone in the crowd of security and health personnel surrounding him. The crowd was too disciplined to suit a revolution. No one could share his feelings and communicate freely on a one to one basis. After his release, he told that the Administration had agreed to let his personal care taker and cook, Gulab Yadav stay with him. JP thought he should not let the poor fellow get interned unnecessarily and suffer the pangs of imprisonment. "Why to curb his freedom which is dear to all?" he told. We, the people around him could not help beyond the administration of medicines and hackneyed reassurances. He had heard enough of us. He needed to discuss the larger issues with his team of national and political leaders; we doctors were a poor substitute – that too in a tense situation with marked restrictions. There was a kind of *'conspiracy of silence'* all around.

I now realize that JP's medical management constituted an important lesson in my career training. Management of a politically important individual is always a sensitive issue. JP's importance exceeded far beyond the usual boundaries meant for routine politicians. He had led a highly explosive national movement which ultimately proved a significant milestone in the history of post-independence India. We could neither be sympathetic nor against the movement. I always felt like riding two horses in a race. Objectivity and honesty would keep us safe. Nonetheless, there existed an inherent risk of miscalculation and misinterpretation. We tended to take decisions based on collective opinions and consensus. In spite of all the sincerity and precautions which we could undertake, we did become victims of political reverberations. We emerged unscathed because of our professional integrity. In the long run, the post-Emergency melodrama which all of us had faced was as valuable an experience as the medical attention to JP.

8.

SHERLOCK HOLMES

Till date, I have not come across a better definition for differential diagnosis of a disease than that given by the celebrated author Sir Arthur Conan Doyle, mouthed through his detective character Sherlock Holmes. Dr. Watson, assistant to Holmes questions him about the identity of the criminal in a story. Holmes replies: "When you have eliminated all which is possible, then whatever remains, however improbable, must be the truth". Not incidentally, that is also the general approach in medicine to diagnose an illness. To diagnose a complex case, one needs to work by exclusion of common causes. Conan Doyle himself was a medical doctor who knew the nuances of the medical profession and tended to translate medical principles into pithy axioms in his detective stories.

I found shades of Sherlock Holmes in Mr. Singh, a senior police officer of the Intelligence Wing of Central Police Services. He was a tall and well-built individual with a pointed moustache. The mixture of grey and black hair in a neatly kept beard provided an aura of maturity to his otherwise fierce looks. He possessed an overpowering personality with deeply set and piercing eyes, which went well with his investigative profession. Ordinary criminals found it hard to stand his interrogation. It was widely believed that a suspect would start pouring out the true confessions the moment he saw Mr. Singh in front of him. Though he was not known particularly for use of any third degree torture, his mere looks and voice were enough! His presence in my chamber was meant for his personal problem rather than to question me. I was therefore relaxed while sitting on the other side of the table. It would have been a different situation during the time of JP's detention! Moreover, that was more than a decade later than the Emergency days, a few years after the turbulent period of Sikh militancy in Punjab.

The gentleman was troubled by the constant presence of dry cough. The symptom was responsible for a sullen mood most of the time. He felt irritated and annoyed while coughing in the presence of others. The embarrassment interfered with his method of interrogations; it diminished his control when he questioned suspects. He also felt that his cough lowered his authority to command his subordinates. Moreover, he felt vulnerable in the presence of senior officers.

In spite of the troublesome symptom, he continued to work for long hours on tough jobs. He used to visit doctors at each place wherever he was posted. He dutifully followed the medical prescriptions which covered the whole gamut of anti-cough medicine. The relief each time was temporary which never lasted beyond the duration of prescribed treatment. Surprisingly, he had never gone through tests beyond the routine x-rays and blood investigations. Specialized investigations were required for correct diagnosis of his illness. Neither he himself, nor any of the physicians he had seen, had insisted upon the need to reach a correct diagnosis.

It was almost one year after his posting at Chandigarh when he first came to consult at the Institute. "Why didn't you care to come earlier in spite of your problematic cough?" I questioned him directly.

"I have hardly stayed in Chandigarh for a continuous period of more than a few days. My duties involve a lot of travel. I am told that the time required for investigations at this place is rather long. Moreover, the process is quite tedious and a large number of tests are usually undertaken", he replied without any hesitation.

"Don't you think that an untreated medical cause of cough would have further worsened the underlying condition?" I continued with my arguments.

"Oh! The cough is there for about five years now. It is almost the same since the beginning, neither less nor more. It is almost a part of my life-style. I am sure that this is likely to last forever. Give me an effective new drug which will keep it suppressed." I noticed a sense of despair as well of twisted logic in his argument.

"Is it not important in your profession to know the nature, and possibly the identity of the criminal before his arrest for damage containment?" I questioned.

"That may not be true in all situations. A culprit who hides from police after committing a crime is unlikely to commit any further crime". He seemed to enjoy the conversation.

"Is it not true that a hidden villain shall perpetrate crime to search for an escape route" I did not wish to lose the argument.

By then, I could judge from his statement that he was fond of detective stories, particularly of Arthur Conan

Doyle. I had also read a few stories by the author. I grabbed the opportunity to bring Sherlock Holmes in our discussion who always insisted upon the need for a correct diagnosis. He was also excited. He told the story of a murder-case about how on his investigations a close family member of the victim was suspected and finally nabbed. The murderer had almost the fool-proof alibi of his absence from the scene. On repeated questioning, one of his (the murderer's) house-maids gave the lead that she did find some mud stuck to his shoes when she cleaned his room in the morning. The murderer's visit to the victim's place could be finally traced through corroborative evidence.

"No chain is stronger than its weakest link", he quoted from Sherlock Holmes.

The icy conversation had now thawed. I explained the similarities between crimes and diseases. They remain hidden until the police investigations or medical tests are able to nail them, as the case may be. I strongly argued in favour of tests required for his diagnosis: "Medical tests proceed almost on the same pattern as police investigation in a highly logical fashion." He was quite reluctant until then. It seemed that he started losing his argument. He claimed to stick to reason throughout his life. He could not object to go through various tests in his own case. 'The search in both cases must proceed in a systematic fashion.'

He was however correct in his assessment that the investigation period lasted longer than necessary. It took about two weeks for him to go through the tests. I could not help in spite of best of my efforts. The waiting periods for some investigations could not be reduced in our crowded hospital with limited resources. He was quite on the edge till the diagnosis could be finally established. He was suffering from *pulmonary sarcoidosis* – a disease which was only rarely diagnosed in India before the turn of the 20th century. It mimicked tuberculosis in several different ways and was therefore kept at the bottom of differential diagnosis. I could not lay blame on doctors who had seen him earlier. Most of them could not have diagnosed the condition. But I must give credit to Sherlock Holmes, who would diagnose the crime with the help of minimal circumstantial evidence.

Mr. Singh responded remarkably well to the treatment. He continued to come for follow up examination and assessment. We had developed mutual appreciation for our approach. We also had a common subject to discuss – the methods of Sherlock Holmes.

In my later years I could conjecture the persona of Mr. Singh in most police officers who reported with an illness to me. They had preference for quick-fix remedies than going through a battery of investigations. But once convinced, they were easier to handle. They generally followed the advice without much fuss. They were also more likely to accept an undiagnosed illness as an unavoidable outcome for want of appropriate investigations. The same was not true for many other categories of patients.

I as an individual have always believed that evidence is crucial for critical analysis to solve a riddle. Once again, I am reminded of another important quote of Sherlock Holmes: "It is a capital mistake to theorize before one has data. Inadvertently, one tends to twist facts to suit theories than theories to suit facts". That remains the basic principle of clinical diagnosis as well as for interpretation of medical research.

9.

THE TWO OUSTEES

Sadhu Ram and Jeeto were two different patients who visited me every 2 to 3 months for over 10 years. They both had similar socio-economic backgrounds – poor, disabled and ill equipped to look after their children. Incidentally, both suffered from similar medical problems as well. Afflicted with chronic respiratory diseases, they always kept on pestering for priority consultation. Though they were quite erratic and non-compliant with medical advice, they used to come to the clinic with clockwork regularity, often left with satisfaction. I learnt during some of my interviews with them, more so during their admissions in the wards, that they both were the original inhabitants of different villages of the region which later transformed to the city of Chandigarh.

I would always spare a few extra minutes to talk to them. I generally enjoyed chatting with them on the merits of rural life. Like most village folks of the region, their talks were humorous in nature. They were frank in their expressions, took a great interest in telling the stories of the land where Chandigarh, 'the city beautiful' was built. Both Jeeto and Sadhu Ram were resentful of the fact that they were thrown away from their original birth-place. They were quite vocal in their criticism about the city especially since the compensations paid to them were generally insignificant.

Chandigarh city was carved out of the land which belonged to several small villages in a large forest area, densely covered with mango trees. The city was needed as the capital of Punjab to accommodate a large number of administrative offices after Lahore was allocated to Pakistan in 1947 after the partition of India. Also, there was a need to rehabilitate displaced people who had moved to Punjab from West Pakistan. The dream city was conceived by Pandit Jawahar Lal Nehru, the first Prime Minister of India. The eminent Swiss-French architect Le Corbusier who was hired for the project had given a distinct shape and character to the city. The overall plan of the city was designed on the theme of an open hand- 'open to give and open to receive'. In 2015, Chandigarh commemorates the 50th anniversary of the death of Le Corbusier, when his legacy is threatened by revelation of his fascist links during the Second World War. The citizens of Chandigarh try to digest those revelations with a degree of sadness.

The architecture of the city or the genius of Le Corbusier meant little for either Sadhu Ram or Jeeto. Sadhu Ram, a small time labourer at a farm had got chronic bronchial asthma. His disease got further complicated by his habit of smoking and irregular treatment. He used to consume all kinds of medicines prescribed to him by the self-styled physicians of his village from time to time. However, whenever his condition deteriorated, he would come to us at the Medical Institute. "How does the beauty of the city help people like me? I am now displaced, an oustee. My children have not even seen the village where I spent my golden days during childhood". He often complained. "But sir, one good thing has happened since then…." Sadhu Ram would say with satisfaction, "I can now get treatment in this big hospital. There was no such thing before the city was built. My father had collapsed in the village without being treated in a hospital…" He at least had some degree of satisfaction with the city.

Sadhu Ram had developed cataracts in both his eyes due to prolonged use of drugs such as corticosteroids for treatment of his chronic asthma. He could hardly see, but carried on as usual without opting for surgery. He would often make light of his disadvantage and dare to crack a joke- "I get greater help from others if I see less". Every time he was offered an operation, he would make an excuse. "What is the need for surgery when I can do my work with this much sight. I do not need to read or write", was his usual reply. One day he revealed that he proposed to get an operation whenever there was a camp for eye-surgery in his village. "It costs little in a camp. Moreover, they also provide free glasses in the camp"

He would visit the hospital to hunt for free medicines from resident doctors. Sale-representatives of different pharmaceutical companies could be commonly seen in the clinics promoting their products and distributing drug samples. Finding little personal use of those drugs, we would often distribute them to needy patients. But expectations increased every time.

Sadhu Ram had invited me several times to visit his village to meet his employer. "Why don't you visit us in our village near Rampur. It is hardly 10-12 *kos* from here.

You will enjoy the village delicacies." Finding it attractive, I along with my wife and son drove one Sunday morning to the farm where he worked. He was quite excited. He took us to the house of his employer – a rich farmer who was also the village *sarpanch*. We were offered thick syrupy tea topped with a thick layer of cream. Not accustomed to that type of drink, I could consume the tea only with great reluctance.

More interestingly, he showed us bee-farming from a very close distance. We were afraid of bees humming around, though he was quite comfortable. There were several wooden boxes with removable top comb-frames used for bee harvesting. Without bothering for protective gear, he would remove a frame with thousands of bees to demonstrate the various types. My son was quite curious to distinguish the queen bee from a worker bee. Afraid of the stings we kept a distance. It is quite astonishing to see photographs and videos of people who can harbour thousands of bees on their bodies.

We were also taken to a small farm with a lot of marigold flowers. The owner was involved in developing different kinds of floriculture in the region. There was a peculiar mix of the traditional and modern types of farming in the area. We also picked up delicious local berries – the '*bers*' and plucked corn. His little children kept running with joy all around us. Without a doubt that proved to be an exciting day. I was reminded of my childhood days when I could easily roam around in the fields which were just a few hundred meters away from my house. I wished I could go around the countryside more frequently than I did.

Several months later, Sadhu Ram got his cataract surgery done at an eye camp held in a town near his village.

He could see better but his asthma had worsened. He very cleverly justified his earlier reluctance for surgery so as to keep his asthma in check. His logic was simple: "Sir, there is a fixed amount of misery which God has allotted to all human beings. If you reduce one problem, the other gets doubled". Considering his example, I could not counter his conclusions.

Slowly, his visits became less frequent. Other patients from his neighbour-hood told me later that he continued to carry on with drugs obtained from dubious sources for some time. Later on, he got bed ridden because of severe pain in his knees. Incidentally, his employer, the more prosperous farmer who had welcomed us with tea in his house had meanwhile died of a sudden heart attack. This had taken away Sadhu Ram's only benefactor and led to his resources being markedly depleted.

Jeeto had a different disease but similar problems. Her financial status was not as bad as of Sadhu Ram but she was a simpleton who could be easily influenced by others. She was constantly looking for advice on treatment of her illness. She would simply believe whatever was told to her. She had tried several formulae as well as concoctions prescribed to her by neighbour-hood friends, the practicing charlatans, village elders and the priests of different cults. After the failure of each trial she would land in the hospital with an acute exacerbation of her illness. Both her lungs were partly destroyed by childhood infections; since then she used to produce a large amount of sputum every day. That was not just annoying but also life threatening especially when accompanied with blood in the sputum.

She believed that the sputum was pooled inside in the lungs and wondered why the same could not be removed at one go. "*Doctor sahib*, why not suck out this muck from my body with machines? Please do anything you like. Do some operation. It does not matter if I die during the operation. But make me well please." Unfortunately, the surgery could not be offered because the disease was far advanced. She also tried to link her problem with her displacement from her original place with a large number of mango trees. "The sweet fragrance of the mango plantation kept me healthy", she always argued. "The mango wood was good to burn in the kitchen. The smoke from that wood acted as a tonic for the lungs. You know that mango wood is preferred for the *havanas* performed for Hindu ceremonies."

One winter night I got a call from the resident on duty in the emergency ward where she had landed with severe respiratory distress. I was told that a '*tantrik*' visiting her village from another town had ensured her radical treatment through mystical means. He took her to a hut, lighted a pyre of dried dung and mango leaves. He had also added a few unknown medicinal roots and some chemicals to the fire to create a dense smoke. She was made to inhale the smoke while he repeatedly slapped her back, chanted magic songs and danced wildly. She violently coughed out secretions in the beginning but landed in trouble within minutes. The *tantric baba* ran away after he noticed her collapsing. She was brought to the hospital by her family in a half-dead state.

Following aggressive management, she slowly recovered from that episode. She had to be kept on mechanical ventilation for a few days. Because of her repeated visits, she had become a familiar patient with the staff of the department. At discharge from the hospital, she had grown weak and lost weight. She expressed her gratitude by blessing every one with good health. She promised to keep away from the magical treatments.

However, one could never rely on a gullible person like Jeeto. Probably she had opted for such a course of treatment one more time. That time she was dead on arrival which made it difficult to fish out a detailed history. Such has been the lure of potentially miraculous cures that even violent assaults would not deter people like Jeeto. More horrendous practices than the simple inhalation of a pungent smoke continue to be used in the hope of a sure cure. It is a never ending story which keeps on recurring again and again. Whenever I see it happen, I am compelled to wonder at the complexities of the human mind.

10.

CULTURE – SHOCK

Berchardt and Alia, a young couple from Denmark happened to visit the Himalayas in the eighties. The boy had developed high fever while trekking a few kilometers beyond Shimla. He was treated at a hospital in Shimla and diagnosed to suffer from pneumonia. The problem was complicated following an air-leak and collapse of the affected lung. The local physician was hesitant to continue with further treatment. There was always a fear of complications or other mishaps. Generally, doctors in peripheral hospitals avoided handling a foreigner for fear of unnecessary questioning by the police. Additionally, there were concerns about uncalled for investigations by other governmental agencies under diplomatic pressures of officials of different embassies. Berchardt was therefore sent to Chandigarh.

Admission in the Emergency ward of the hospital was a shock for the couple. We had always thought that the Institute was highly sophisticated. But the Danes were not impressed. The Danes considered it smelly, crowded and noisy. It was quite primitive by their standards. However, there was no alternative; neither could they escape nor could we improve conditions. As per the requirements of his medical diagnosis, a chest-tube was inserted for drainage of pus. He felt relieved after some time but a prolonged period of care was essential. Hospitalization was therefore required for administration of antibiotics and stabilization of his condition.

Stay in the Emergency ward lasted a trying period of a day and a half. There was a continuous movement of new patients. Berchardt had at least a bed to lie upon. Alia had hardly a place to rest. She was quite exhausted. Finally she chose to straighten her back on the floor. The prying eyes of other patients made them wary of the place. The resident on duty heaved a sigh of relief when night descended. Soon they both slipped into sleep.

There was an entirely different scene in the morning. They were quite cheerful after a restful sleep. That was perhaps the first painless night in the last week. By then, they were also conditioned to the *primitive surroundings*. Moreover, the others in the ward were not concerned with the presence of *aliens* anymore. By afternoon, Berchardt could be transferred to an independent room in the Private Wards. This greatly eased the situation.

The next shock came in the morning of third day. I along with my resident doctors was making routine rounds in the private ward. Suddenly, there we heard a shriek – a student-nurse, Bela came running out of the room of Danish boy. She was rather hysterical as if she had seen a ghost. We were quite disturbed at the possibility of a serious mishap. The Sister-in-charge of the ward took her to a side-room to calm her down. It took a long time before the details became known.

What Bela had seen was not a ghost but Alia, who by then had also come out of the room to look for the reason of the shriek. She was clad only in her scant bikini dress. She had been getting ready for a bath but did not bother to lock the room from inside as she did not expect anyone to disturb her privacy. There was nothing unusual in what she wore as per her norms. On the other hand, it was a highly shocking experience for our student-nurse who considered it highly immodest or shameful. It was an entirely different matter that the nursing student did not bother to knock on the door before going in.

The couple was greatly upset but did not understand the problem. I tried to explain the reason which they must have partly understood. The language was a great barrier. Their understanding of my explanations was marginal at best. Somehow the essence of the argument was conveyed that the dress which she wore was not usual in our milieu. They felt sorry and promised to be more careful in the future.

The boy responded to treatment faster than expected and improved within a few days. With little money in hand and no credit cards, they were very worried regarding the hospital bills. They wanted to contact the Embassy for help. The meager bill came as a great surprise to them. They were full of praise for the hospital when they went; Alia and Bela had also befriended each other!

Experience with patients from abroad has not been necessarily pleasant every time. It was entirely a different experience to handle John Griffth who was referred by a physician from *Kullu* for treatment of his worsening breathlessness. He was a forty plus gentleman who used to smoke heavily in the past. He was accompanied by two

Indian teenagers from the Kullu region. His lungs were grossly emphysematous. Voluminous in size, the lungs would hardly move with respiration. He was restless, delirious and talked incoherently. We feared that he could collapse any time.

He was immediately put on oxygen and other necessary treatments were simultaneously instituted. He settled over the next 24 hours to his *baseline breathlessness*. We thought it prudent to stabilize him further before sending him back to *Kullu* or wherever he wanted to go. Surprisingly, he wanted to leave the hospital immediately in spite of our advice to stay for a few more days. He told us a story which we found a little difficult to believe. He along with a few friends from some European country had come to India about a year before. His money, the passport and other documents were all stolen. His friends had deserted him and went back. He went to the police, who were not at all helpful. On the other hand, the police took bribe to allow him to stay, sans a passport and visa. We wanted to confirm the facts from the boys who had brought him to Chandigarh. They had already disappeared from the scene.

What followed thereafter was more of a night-mare. I politely tried to inquire about the passport number or police report, etc. He started arguing in an almost abusive manner. He blamed every one of us for detaining him forcibly in the hospital. That was not a delirious state any more. Repeatedly, he shouted that he would complain to the Counsellor of the Embassy. We had no other choice than to inform the Medical Superintendent who tried to contact the local police station in *Kullu*. He did not succeed in his efforts till the evening.

Next morning, we received two policemen who had come from *Kullu* looking for Griffth. They had a different account to tell. We were told that Griffth was engaged in an illegal drug racket. Not wishing to go back to his country, he tended to ditch the police on one or the other pretext. No one from his family from his country had ever contacted the police of the State. He was accused of over-staying his tourist-visa. Police also suspected his involvement in narcotic smuggling. He was held initially but released later at the intervention of a local *'guru'* who used to take care of him. He had promised to the police that he would soon return to Delhi for his onward journey back home. The gentlemanly promise was never kept.

The police was tipped off by a local practitioner whom Griffth had consulted for his breathlessness. Rather than asking for medicine for his illness, he had been pestering the doctor to get him cocaine. He was said to have even threatened to get the practitioner eliminated through the local drug mafia. Greatly fearful, the doctor informed the police.

"We work in very difficult conditions. Whenever we wish to take action, we face tremendous political and diplomatic pressures. Dealing with foreigners, especially the Whites, is not easy", said the police constable. I was told that a number of foreign tourists who came for the drugs always tended to overstay. They made multiple excuses to escape eviction. They would either conceal or destroy their passports. The police were hardly equipped to handle the issue. Concerned Embassies were equally clueless and tended to ignore or overlook the issue.

These type of tourists frequently disappeared in the local *ashrams*. A number of small-time *gurus* and drug-dens had also cropped-up in the valley to earn from the trade. To my great relief, the police took Griffth back to *Kullu*. I do not know whether he was taken to the prison or to the *"Ashram"* of his guru. I felt sorry that his future was not very bright in either case.

The Kullu valley is famous for its magnificent forests covered with deodar and pine trees. The numerous apple orchards have made it the fruit basket of Himachal Pradesh. It has an ancient history dating back to the time of the Budha who was said to have preached to the local people. Emperor Ashoka had installed one of his famous *stupas* at that site, which was subsequently removed to Delhi by one of the Mughal rulers. There are both Hindu temples and Budhist monastries which attract a large number of devotees and visitors. The city itself is famous for its annual Hindu festival of *Dasehra* which marks the day of victory of Lord *Rama* over the demon king, *Ravana*. The plight of *Kullu* being eroded by drug-trafficking has been a matter of great concern.

I had a more satisfying experience with a senior functionary belonging to an American medical association. Richard Paul from USA was a member of the faculty for a large international conference which we had held at Chandigarh. During travel, the poor Dr. Paul developed an extremely painful swelling of one of his finger-tips probably due to an in-growing nail. Throughout the flight, he needed repeated administration of pain relieving drugs. The flight was rather long and he had already taken an overdose of analgesic drugs. When he landed at Chandigarh, he was received at the airport by a member of the reception-team. Without taking notice of any of the greetings, the first thing he demanded, "Take me straight to Dr. Jindal."

"Sir, we shall move to the hotel where a room is reserved for you. You can take rest and make yourself comfortable. It is late in the evening to move to the venue. Dr. Jindal will see you there in the morning when the conference starts."

"No. First I need to go to the hospital. I have got severe pain."

That was rather scary lest it be a heart attack. No one wanted a tragedy to happen at the very beginning of the Conference being organized with great fanfare. He was immediately made comfortable in the waiting taxi and moved to the Institute. It was on the way that he was able to narrate his problem. There was a small collection of pus which needed an incision.

I was informed of the issue before he reached the hospital. I did not wish drainage to be done in the routine Emergency OPD. I thought he deserved to be handled as an honoured-guest by one of our senior surgeons. Regretfully, the first surgeon I asked was not very helpful. Quietly, I requested the second surgeon, who happily obliged.

Dr. Paul felt instant relief on incision. "It seems I have got a second life", he commented. He profusely thanked the surgeon. He felt highly obliged for the surgeon's help. He was so happy that he gave the surgeon an invitation for a complimentary visit to USA to participate in a meeting of the organization– all at their cost. Later, the surgeon who had earlier refused to help expressed his regrets to me over the entire episode. He had several excuses to offer. I thought he was a bit peeved to miss the free trip. But I could not help; it was his choice.

11.

'MORRIE' OF PUNJAB

Dr. Chaudhry's struggle with his illness was no different than that of Morrie who lived far away in the United States. Morrie Schmartz was a college professor whose struggle with death from a progressive and disabling neurological disease was immortalized in 'Tuesdays with Morrie' by his student Mitch Albom. I did not train with Dr. Chaudhry as a student for any length of time. I met him during a 'Continuing Medical Education Program' at the medical college. Thereafter, I kept myself abreast of his condition on a regular basis. Like Morrie, Dr. Chaudhry suffered from a chronic form of progressive muscle weakness. Though I am no Mitch Albom, I have tried to present the story of his life as perceived by me during the time I interacted with him.

His was a life of remarkable courage and conviction. Even now, I do not hesitate to quote his example to a patient who feels low or depressed because of a chronic and debilitating illness. His attitude to his life, devotion to his family and dedication to work were all exemplary. Above all, he had made major contributions to his department, as well as to the subject of medicine. Work was an act of faith for him. He never let his physical disability over-shadow his ambitions and zeal. His contributions to science may not match to that of Stephen Hawking, who has suffered from a more disabling neurological disease, but his life story certainly did. His life was a constant battle with his disease which he always faced with boldness. "Do not deceive yourself with denials of disease and death. Accept the reality of inevitability", he always said.

Dr. Chaudhry had moved to India in 1973 after a few years' stint in the medical profession in the United States. He had worked in different positions at different hospitals in Houston and Seattle. He left the green pastures of America to serve his country; the decision was also partly influenced by recognition of the early symptoms of illness while he was still in America. "I thought it better to be with my family in India in the later years of life, more importantly to contribute whatever I have with me", he told me once.

I met Dr. Chaudhry for the first time at the medical college when I went there to participate in a teaching program. I was a student at that time, pursuing my post-graduation in medicine. Dr. Chaudhry had recently joined the faculty of the medical college. I distinctly remember the scene when he entered the lecture theatre. I was sitting in a middle row, several steps higher than the floor level. Dr. Chaudhry walked up to that row and sat near me. He could walk with ease, though with a mild degree of waddling. "Perhaps the new teacher has sprained his ankle" I thought. The persistence of the gait ever thereafter remained a subject of inquisitiveness among the students. It was much later that the problem became known to others.

Dr. Chaudhry introduced himself and initiated the dialogue with me. I was a little reticent in the beginning but the ice was soon broken. He had a knack to make one comfortable. We talked on several issues related to medical education. That was just the beginning. Our mutual interaction continued for several years to come. We had several common issues which kept us mutually engaged.

Dr. Chaudhry took great interest in his classes. The regularity with which he participated in different academic sessions was rather a source of envy for many others. Generally, he was the first to arrive for a class. Above all, he kept himself engaged in one or the other project to remain busy in the otherwise free time. He encouraged his students to work on small research proposals, in addition to their thesis work. I emulated his example and took up a project myself when I was only a second year junior resident at Chandigarh. That was how I could achieve a few publications, even though small in scope in the very beginning of my medical career. This greatly helped me to make an early dent in medical research – a field which I relished for the rest of my professional life.

In the years to come, his disease gradually progressed. His walking speed became slower. Soon he required the help of a stick. It was around that time that he encouraged me to join the Faculty of a medical college than settle in practice. I, like most other residents, wished to join Cardiology. He strongly motivated me to opt for a 'less developed' *specialty*. "You will be able to make your mark in a subject new to the people in India", he told me once. I was hesitant in the beginning but later decided to accept the bait.

Pulmonology in India at that time was mostly synonymous with the specialty of tuberculosis. I took the challenge to upgrade the specialty to that of super-specialty level. I was able to introduce *fiberoptic bronchoscopy* which was rather new to India in the late seventies. I began with my work in the *Oto-Rhino-Laryngology* ward on *tracheostomized* patients of laryngeal cancer. Soon I could expand the *broncho-endoscopy* services to comfortably undertake procedures on all kinds of patients. Thereafter, I was able to introduce assisted respiratory support for patients of respiratory failure. I finally succeeded in my efforts to introduce the Post-doctoral Fellowship program (DM) in Pulmonary Medicine. Incidentally, the PGI was not only the first to start but also remained the only center for that Program for the next twenty years.

Finding it difficult to cope with a stick, Dr. Chaudhry soon became wheel-chair bound. That did not hamper his interest in any manner. He continued to attend his office, would never miss a class or an out-patient clinic. "Who knows? I might need the same in the years to come. I shall like to die in the hands of my own people" Dr. Chaudhry remarked in a lighter vein on one day. Intensive care in those days was primarily taken care of by the anesthesiologists. At the Institute in Chandigarh, my department became one of first where an Intensive Care Unit was attached to a Department of Pulmonary Medicine.

I used to talk to Dr. Chaudhry off and on to decide on management of a difficult case. At times, there were differences in our view-points. He was somewhat conservative in his approach to the diagnostic and therapeutic interventions, especially for chronic illnesses. His patients greatly admired his advice. I was more enthusiastic and mostly in favour of an aggressive approach. The differences in attitude were frequently responsible for disagreement and debate. But, he had a significantly larger experience than me. To his great credit, he would often yield to my viewpoint with an advice to be cautious and careful. "One should not look doubtful while caring for a patient" he often said. In most cases, it worked well.

I remember a patient with advanced chronic lung disease. He was an obvious candidate for long-term support for his respiration. The respiratory support at home could be provided with a mechanical ventilator. Neither the device nor the expertise required for such a situation was available in India at that time. Moreover, there was no known example in the region to follow. I thought to experiment with the use of a portable ventilator but had no first-hand experience. I thought Dr. Chaudhry might have used the same In USA. I called for his advice. He was taken by surprise. He was completely against that costly treatment in the absence of appropriate resources in the country. "You will be unnecessarily blamed for a failure. It will be worse in case of a complication or a mishap", he forcefully argued. The patient was rich and ready to experiment with any advanced treatment. On my persuasive reasoning, the patient accepted and opted for the domiciliary ventilation. The experiment proved to be fruitful. The patient had lived on for a few more years afterwards.

It is interesting to observe that now over the years I myself tend to be more conservative. Frequently I express my reservations on invasive procedures about which my younger colleagues would not think twice. On the other hand, the wider availability of medical technology and expertise has made us wise and bold. I therefore do not impose my decisions on younger colleagues of my team, most of the time. This I believe is an important principle in case of collective care. I tend to be cautious partly for fear of malpractice litigations which were practically unknown in the past. It is rather enigmatic that doctors are compelled to practice defensive medicine.

We also had plenty of subjects of common interest to talk about. Because of his illness, Dr. Chaudhry would spend most of his time in his office while in the hospital. He was quite a bookworm in reading medical books and journals. Whenever a bit tired of reading, he would call me on phone. Besides the socio-political issues, we had a number of general as well as personal issues to deliberate. Occasionally, he would ask my opinion for his problem or a possible complication. Largely, he avoided the mention of his illness or disability thereof.

"What are the common causes of headache", Dr. Chaudhry asked me once. I gave a full list of causes ranging from tension, fatigue, anxiety, sinusitis and poor vision to specific neurological diseases such as migraine and cluster headache. He kept on listening until I came to the more serious reasons such as bleeding in the brain, the tumours and retention of carbon dioxide due to respiratory fatigue. That was the break point. I was taken aback as he abruptly interrupted the discussion. He clarified that he was seeking the cause of his own headache which was there since the morning. I tried to dilute the seriousness of causes in my exhaustive list. "But sir, some…., perhaps many of these causes, are rather infrequent. Your headache is attributable more to your fatigue", I tried to explain. The subject was conveniently dropped. His headache had already gone.

Retrospectively, whenever I tried to reflect upon that discussion, I felt that he had already developed an early, incipient respiratory failure due to respiratory muscle fatigue. I had unnecessarily given him the concession of being a doctor. Doctors frequently commit errors in their approach to differential diagnosis of illnesses which affect them or people very close to them. Factually, the list of causes responsible for different problems remains the same irrespective of the importance of the man.

Dr. Chaudhry's condition deteriorated further after a few months or about a year. He had started with recurrent headaches, fatigue and sweating. Several of his friends had advised him to seek an early retirement to avoid exertion of daily work. He did not wish to sit idle at home. He often said that he wanted to be with his patients till he dies. He was also hard-pressed to continue in service for family needs.

Everyone had known of the end but it came sooner than expected. One summer morning I received a call from his home that he had collapsed while getting ready to come for work. He was taken to his Hospital Emergency where he was found to be deeply unconscious. He remained on cardio-respiratory support in the Intensive Care Unit for about a week. But all efforts at resuscitation proved futile.

The trauma of his death remained with me for quite a while. His demise was a big setback for his family and the medical college he served. It also created a void in my own professional life. I missed his sane advice. Seeing disease and death every day, I was quite conditioned. I thought I could carry on with my work in the face of tragic and trying conditions. Dr. Chaudhry's death had proved me wrong, at least for a temporary period.

12.

THE AMERICAN DREAM

My selection for the International Fogarty Fellowship proved to be a major mile-stone in my career. It provided me with a unique opportunity to see the practice of medicine in the West. In addition, I could relish first-hand, the experiences of living life in America, the dream-land for a large number of people from all over the world. Incidentally, in the early seventies when a large number of doctors had migrated to the United States, it was commonly believed that a resident missing suddenly from the morning rounds must have moved to America, in all likelihood! The Indian Governmental had banned the qualifying ECFMG examination for entry to the Residency Program in America, from being held in India. People used to travel to neighbouring countries to bypass the Indian ban. Concerns of the sixties and the seventies about the *brain-drain from India* slowly diminished and soon vanished.

I chose Seattle in the United States for my Fellowship at the University of Washington. That was primarily a research assignment for about a year and a half, without any clinical responsibilities in the hospital. I was not too keen to see patients in the clinics. I did have a large clinical exposure to and experience with patients back home. In any case, I was not licensed to indulge in clinical practice in America. I did however take care to spend some time in the clinical wards, as well as to attend the different teaching sessions.

The absence of a license was not enough to keep me away from clinical medicine. I could hardly stay away from giving opinions. However, there was no scope of prescribing any medicine. Like in India, I was frequently required for 'non-official' and 'casual' consultations sought primarily by friends and acquaintances for their medical problems. The pattern was similar for people from India and Pakistan. Several times it seemed that differences between us and the Pakistanis were rather few except that we were vegetarian in our eating habits. Throughout our stay in Seattle, we purchased the Indian grocery from a shop owned by a Pakistani migrant. There was no Indian shop around at that time. My advice on medical matters was mostly theoretical. The case of Mr. Jain was different from all others.

I met Jain and his family at a small function organized by a common friend working at the University. I, along with my wife Umesh and our 3 year old son were in search of friends in the *alien* surroundings of a foreign land. After leaving the hustle and bustle of a busy hospital in India, Umesh was particularly lonely in the absence of any significant work to keep her busy. Fellow-Indians, most of them working with Boeing, were rather few in Seattle in the early eighties. Microsoft was not particularly known, but the Jains were there for several years. Mrs. Jain at her home had little to do after her routine house-hold activities. Above all, they missed the comfort of a medical opinion, like that in India. In need of each other, there soon developed a good rapport between us based on mutual trust and shared frustrations.

Jain had come to Seattle after quitting a frustrating job he had held in the Forestry department of Uttar Pradesh in the late seventies. As per his version, he was fed up with the highly corrupt system of administration in his department back home in India. He could neither stop poaching nor prevent the illegal felling of trees in the forests under his care. The local forest mafia was protected by powerful politicians and criminals. He was repeatedly transferred from one position to the other. At times, he even faced threats of physical assault or injury. Besides his aged parents, he had a wife and two children to look after. Somehow, he got a chance to move to America with the help and sponsorship of an old friend. He immediately grabbed the opportunity.

In America, Jain worked very hard to make both ends meet. Finally he succeeded in his ambitions to live a comfortable life. But he suffered from chronic asthma which troubled him all the time. He always tended to deny the severity or even the presence of his illness. His wife was quite upset with his denials. She could not see him suffer all the time. On the other hand, he was too egoistic to accept that he had asthma. He would dismiss his problem as inconsequential: "I have faced great many hardships in India. This problem of a little cough is recent. It shall soon disappear after 2-3 days of steam inhalation and gargles". He was generally averse to the use of drugs, preferred to underplay the degree of his discomfort and disability. He was also a strong believer in homeopathic and natural treatments which were not easily available in America.

One could hear whistling noises emanating from his chest while sitting in his company. Not infrequently, the musical, rumbling sounds, echoed like the subdued barking of a pup or mewing of a cat. He was blissfully unaware that others in his company not only heard the wheezing sounds but felt uncomfortable. It was certainly difficult for a person like me who knew of their importance, to ignore their presence. After taking his wife into confidence, who was pleased to avail my voluntary assistance, I decided to broach the subject one day.

"Doesn't your asthma limit your physical capacity to do work and move around?" I purposely posed a direct question to him. Though startled, he immediately retorted with his standard explanation: "I do not have asthma. This little rattling in the throat has happened due to an early morning walk. The air was rather cold. I am quite healthy otherwise." He was partly correct in his assessment but his denial of asthma was rather weak. After a few more questions, he came out of his shell of false defences. He soon confided in me that asthma bothered him quite a bit. "I cannot help. I do visit the doctor whenever the problem gets worse. At each visit, I am provided with a long list of medicines including the prescription of an inhaler. Moreover, the doctor warns me about with a list of potential complications of asthma and possible side-effects of medicine".

"But that is what a doctor is supposed to do to help you manage your asthma" I tried to reason with him.

"The doctor is always impassive. His tone is monotonous. It is more legal than genuine assurance. Each time, I get completely off-set, disappointed. I get discouraged than develop any degree of confidence in the treatment" he replied.

He gave a long commentary on American doctors and their methods of handling patients. "They are harsh, impersonal, unsympathetic, business-like and unconcerned with patients' emotions. Their only motive is to charge the Insurance to make money. Moreover, they tend to ensure protection from legal problems by exaggerating disease complications."

I was shocked at his conclusive statements. I completely disagreed with his charges but kept quiet. The time was not ripe to enter into an argument on the quality of medical care in the United States. His opinion did not match my own assessment of US physicians I had met. They were sincere, but transparent. They worked in a different legal frame-work but generally followed standard treatment protocols. True to the system of medical practice, an American doctor left the option of decision-making to his patient. An Indian doctor on the other hand, tended to make decisions on behalf of the patient.

I have known the frustration of tired patients who do not get well in spite of continued treatments. Not uncommonly, one starts accusing the doctor for failure of a treatment. More than ever before, we in India are now bitten by the same bug – the fear of malpractice suits. It is rather intriguing to note that the Consumer Protection Act in India has become the root cause of defensive medical practice. It has been also responsible for increased health care costs. There is loss of a genuine doctor-patient relationship. The differences in medical practice between America and India have fast disappeared.

Another reason for Jain's distrust was his nostalgia for the country he had left in search of the American dream. The decision to come to America was not made by choice but was almost forced upon him by circumstances. First generation Indian migrants used to compare everything in USA with that in India. Several of them like Jain moved to USA for better incomes and a more conducive working environment. But they missed the warmth of an extended family. The informal personal relationships of Indian system were missing in a different society. There was a little sweet India hidden somewhere in their hearts. During the rest of my US stay as well as subsequent visits over the next 30 years, I met many of the non-resident Indians who similarly missed India. Some of them also expressed preferences to either move to India or do something for their motherland. The same could not be necessarily said of second and third generation Indians born and brought up in the USA –they were as American as other American citizens.

Deciding to be patient with Mr. Jain, I took my time to react. I agreed with him that the personal touch of a physician was significantly less than during Osler's time. Osler, also described as the 'father of modern medicine' was the first to introduce bed-side clinical training in medical teaching. He had always insisted upon the importance of the physician-patient relationship.

"Management strategies get complicated due to several extraneous considerations. But these issues do not affect the quality of treatment. On the other hand, patients are sometimes unable to communicate their problems", I tried to rationalize.

"It is the duty of a doctor to let his patient enter into a helpful dialogue", he asserted. "The doctor must sympathize with his patient. Assurance is essential for successful treatment".

I would have used the term 'empathize' instead of sympathize. That however was not the core issue. The conversation went on with arguments and counter-arguments, for and against physicians and their methods of interacting with their patients. No conclusion could be reached, but the barrier was broken. I considered the experience as a successful experiment in the management of a tough patient.

He was a hard nut to crack, no doubt. Rarely, does a doctor enter into such a long whamming talk as I did with him. Perhaps it also worked as a stimulus for me, as it kept my mind logged on to clinical medicine during that period of *dog-experiments* in research laboratories. The clinical rounds I used to attend there were nowhere similar to the rounds in India. The daily bedside discussions in our hospital at Chandigarh were lively and full of charisma. On the other hand, the bed-side rounds in the US hospital were more professional and business like. Sometimes, it did seem that what Jain had said was not entirely untrue. Possibly, the differences were cultural in nature. An American patient would not like his problem to be discussed in the open during the ward round. We in India take a lot more liberties with our patients. Factually an Indian patient seems to enjoy deliberations about his/ her illness. It is a matter of pride for a patient to boast to others if his problems are discussed in depth on the rounds or in a bed-side class.

One simple example of different cultural responses was narrated to me by one of my senior colleagues in USA. Once on the rounds, he stopped to say hello to an elderly individual admitted with abdominal distension. "Hello, old man! Did you move your bowels today?" the doctor asked. The patient curtly replied: "Thanks for calling me old, taking off my shorts in public". The doctor quickly apologized and hurried away. An Indian elderly patient back home would not be unduly disturbed as being addressed as an *old man*. On the contrary, he might feel happy at the respect shown by the doctor.

My friend soon started with his drug inhalers prescribed by his past doctor on a regular basis. Inhalation therapy though known since ancient time had been only recently introduced in modern medicine. Even though the earliest documented evidence of the prescription of inhalational forms of herbs for different treatments dates back to the *Eber's papyri* (c.1550 B.C.), yet in the 1980s, inhalation was just growing out of its infancy. Newer inhalers and add-on devices were slow to enter the market. Patients were not yet used to inhalational treatment. "I hope that I shall not get addicted to inhalers", Jain had asked. "Do not worry. There is no narcotic or habituating drug in an inhaler. It is only a device for drug administration" I explained the merits of using an inhaler. I calmly explained the technique of inhalation to my friend who quickly learnt the same. He felt better with the treatment which he had earlier dismissed as rubbish. Sadly, the misconception of 'addiction' to inhalers still remains a stumbling block to efficient management of asthma.

On his own admission, he had never felt better than after a few week of treatment. He greatly appreciated the improvement in his well-being. He no more felt fatigued or exhausted after the day's work. His wife and elder daughter were grateful for my advice. Near *Diwali*, on the day of the *Karva Chauth* fast, they invited us along with another Indian couple to join them in the evening for dinner after the fasting was over. *Karva Chauth* fast, fervently observed in North India by married women for the welfare and long lives of their husbands, could be 'broken' only after the sighting of the moon. However, on that cloudy October night, the moon was nowhere to be seen and seemed to play a hide and seek game with us. We, the three husbands, together made repeated visits in Jain's car to nearby locations to search for the moon to earn our dinner. It was after a long time that the fast was finally broken after a friend in Tacoma, a nearby town, telephonically confirmed the sighting of the moon!

13.

PICKWICK PAPERS

Sumer Singh was an extremely fat man who weighed over 110 kg, almost equivalent to the weight of two adult men. That would be termed as *'morbidly obese'* in medical terminology. The chair on which he sat in front of me was grossly inadequate to accommodate his bulk. I was apprehensive that the chair which was making noises under his weight might collapse. Fortunately, the chair was made of tin and extremely strong. It took time for the patient to control his breathing after walking to my room; he was still panting when he moved in the examination room.

I had already guessed his illness. Yet I chose to ask him about the problems he had to which he replied rather bluntly: "I do not have any illness. I have come to satisfy my wife who insisted that I should see you here".

"You must be joking. I thought you were quite breathless when you moved in. Are you sure you are well?" I questioned.

"Oh! I am quite well. It is because of my weight that I get breathless. Did not I settle down after a little rest?" He had very few complaints of his own except that he found it difficult to climb up and down from the first floor, where he lived. Fearing that the purpose of the visit to the hospital might be lost, his wife took over. She had a long list of complaints which she quickly went through.

"Doctor, my husband is sleepy all the time. He falls asleep even while having a conversation. It has become difficult to discuss any issue with him. He snores very loudly. It is almost impossible to sleep near him. I have to shift to a separate room at night. My grown-up son is very disturbed. He is highly resentful. I am afraid of his rebellious behaviour. He keeps on asking me to go to a doctor for his father's treatment." She spoke almost uninterruptedly: "I had to use all my powers to bring him here. It has not been an easy task. Doctor, please do something to help."

I wondered how I could help such an unwilling patient. It did not require any degree of intelligence or imagination to make a diagnosis. But the problem could not be solved with a mere talk or prescription of some drugs. *Morbid obesity* is a disease by itself. The presence of excessive sleepiness makes it worse. Medical students always found the clinical syndrome as particularly interesting. It had also been the subject of numerous jokes. "I shall straightway seek a divorce if I my husband sleeps when I talk", a girl had remarked after the subject was first introduced to us in medical school.

The syndromic conglomeration of obesity, snoring and excessive sleep had drawn the interest of authors even before that of doctors. Charles Dickens described a characteristic picture of the syndrome in his celebrated novel '*The Posthumous Papers of the Pickwick Club*'. The medical term '*Pickwickian Syndrome*' was aptly coined after the character, the fat boy Joe who would sit at the gate on a stool and repeatedly lapse into sleep. Mr. Wardle for whom Joe worked gleefully mentioned to his surprised friend Samuel

Pickwick: "….he's always asleep. Goes on errands fast asleep, and snores as he waits at table." Joe would also consume large quantities of food. Pickwick himself was depicted as physically bulky and stout, but the medical syndrome fitted the character of Joe rather than that of Pickwick – the main protagonist of the *Pickwick Club*.

Sumer Singh enjoyed his sleep as well as his food with equal fervour. He was blissfully ignorant of his gluttonous habits. He attributed excessive sleep to fatigue due to work pressure, though his work was entirely sedentary in nature. His office was located on the ground floor of the building in which he lived. He would somehow come down to his office in the morning and go back up in the late evening. There was no need to commute anywhere else except for an occasional function. Driving was out of question. His car driver always found it taxing to take him out whenever it was required. He would start snoring the moment he settled in the back seat. It was a real exercise to wake him up and get him out of the car at the destination.

The constant nagging by his wife had made him seek medical opinion. In spite of her being a well-built individual, there was no similarity between the physical make-up of husband and wife. She was a strong woman the tranquillity of whose face was disturbed by circumstances. Their grown-up son had started complaining about the disturbance caused by papa's snoring. At night he could not stay in his study located adjacent to his father's bed-room. Moreover, he found it difficult to invite his friends at home for fear of exposing the embarrassing habits of his father. It was not easy for the mother to convince the young teenager every time. Unlike his mother, the son had no real inhibition in talking to his father. He was becoming more aggressive every day.

Sumer Singh finally agreed to come to the hospital more to please his family than to see to his own real needs. After all, he was only in his mid –forties and hoped to live a long life. He was a pleasant person who enjoyed making jokes about himself and his weight. He expressed his helplessness to control his snoring. He jovially shared a joke about a news-item he had recently read. A lady in the United States had sought divorce from her husband on account of his loud snoring which disturbed her sleep. "What disgusting behaviour? Asking for a divorce on such a petty issue! People in the West have no respect for the sacred relationship between a husband and his wife." He was unstoppable in his judgment. "We must not let a similar situation develop in India. The rotten practices of the West must be necessarily avoided in India." He continued expressing his sentiments during much of the time he spent with me. I did not wish to contradict his statements on that issue. I had the interest of his family in my mind more than the need to express my views on the rights of women. I was sure that counter arguments would not work in the given circumstances. But it did seem to me that there was an imperceptible threat of separation in his mind.

It was not simple to manage the problems of Sumer Singh and his family. None of the medical issues could be resolved with mere administration of medicines as he wished. Like most obese patients, he was also on the lookout for magical herbs or drugs that would relieve him of the malady, without effecting a change in diet or life-style. He was not prepared to use the standard treatment with a non-invasive ventilator - a mechanical device with a tight fitting facial mask which provided pressurised air throughout sleep. In all fairness to him, therapies for weight reduction are generally poorly effective. It requires a herculean effort to avoid high calorie foods. The over-abundance of such items at his home made it worse to achieve the goals.

Thereafter, he was more regular in his follow-up visits. He had seen a dietician once or twice in between. A surgeon was also consulted to do some miracle-therapy though the idea was soon abandoned by both himself and his wife. Every time he came, he expressed his helplessness due to the inherent difficulties involved in the treatment. He had practically resigned himself to the fate. The son had meanwhile moved to a hostel. He had stopped grumbling whenever he accompanied his father to the hospital.

If 'well begun is half done' then 'poorly begun is undone'! After a few years of his initial visit, he was brought to the hospital in frank respiratory failure. He seemed to have further added to his weight which was partly due to accumulation of lot of water in his body. His medical condition was hopeless and irretrievable. He remained in and out of the hospital for variable periods during his shortened life-span thereafter.

While writing about Sumer Singh, I was pleasantly reminded of the story of a young European lady Natasha, settled in Australia. I was taken to her house in Sydney by a friend during one of my visits there for a medical conference. She wanted to show me some excellent pieces of stitch-work in which my wife was particularly interested. Natasha suffered from bronchial asthma for which she wished to seek a few clarifications regarding the life-style changes required to cope with her problems. The issues were rather trivial in nature and she was quite satisfied after a counselling session. She also told me about her past history of obesity and how she had overcome it. It was a remarkable story of determination, not just interesting but clearly inspiring. That was in stark contrast to the sad story of Sumer Singh.

Natasha had also weighed over a hundred kilos in her teens. She had become the butt of jokes for fellow students in her school. Her repeated attempts to lose weight by restricting food had failed. The few kilos which she used to loose after following a starvation diet over a few weeks would be back within the next month. After a lot of coaxing by some of her friends, she finally opted for radical surgical management. The gastrointestinal bye-pass surgery involved resection of a part of her intestines. Thereafter, she could retain only some of what she ate.

She succeeded shedding several kilos of fat. As a result, the skin over her limbs started to hang loose. Multiple sessions of surgical resection of the loose skin-folds were done on an almost six-monthly basis. After a long and punishing period, she turned into a slim and beautiful girl. She needed to regularly consume a number of vitamins and food supplements but the fear of weight gain had gone. She was busy with her stitch- work to earn a good living. Moreover, she looked forwards to the future with a great hope. She had also found a handsome partner in her college. A series of photographs which she showed me were clear proof of her tenacity and success.

A doctor friend at Chandigarh proved to be an even more glaring example than that of Natasha. He shed over a third of his body weight of almost ninety kilos in less than a year. In the past, I had seen that kind of example mostly in advertisements in magazines or the internet. He has been a clear outlier. He achieved the goal simply by staying away from food with a strict diet plan. He had made a sudden cold-turkey decision one day after casual discussion on bariatric surgery with a surgeon colleague. The surgeon told him jocularly: "Why not seal the mouth with a surgical suture than the stomach?" He took the joke with all seriousness. He used a determination seal on his mouth, stopping all foods with high calorie values. He was intelligent enough to calculate his requirements for essential food items and other supplements, in consultation with a dietician. His prescription for others remained simple: "Say 'shut-up' to your mind whenever it asks for more. Never become subservient to your tongue". He maintained an ideal weight thereafter.

It is not my purpose to enter into a debate on the problems and management of obesity or the *Pickwickian Syndrome.* I do not recommend either the tough surgical route through which Natasha had gone or a starvation diet as the ideal approach. Management plans are generally different for different patients. Major advances have taken place to make the available treatment options for obesity safe and effective. But the outcome of a treatment depends significantly on the attitude and determination of the patient. The cases of Sumer Singh and Natasha were poles apart. Sumer Singh was casual and carefree with his plans and neglected the medical advice at the cost of his health. On the other hand, Natasha and the doctor friend were deeply committed to treatment. Sumer Singh failed while both of the others achieved success.

We do not know what happened to Dicken's Joe in the long run. But we do know the fate of possibly the first patient of *Pickwickian Syndrome* described in 1956[*] in the original study on the syndrome - more than a century later after the publication of Pickwick Papers. A businessman who used to play poker once a week had similar characteristics as those of Joe. On a crucial occasion while playing poker, he was dealt a hand of "three aces and two kings - a full house." The poker-player could not take advantage of that opportunity because he had dropped off to sleep. *"A few days later he entered…hospital"* was said in that report.

*   Burwell et al. American Journal of Medicine, 1956. Vol 21 (5).

14.

GOD'S OWN PEOPLE

There is a large group of patients who cannot afford to pay for their treatment. They get themselves listed in the 'poor-free' category of patients in the hospital. That is generally true for most public hospitals in India. One must admit that the treatment given to this group of patients may not be ideal as per the standard professional guidelines. But one can achieve significant success in a most cases in spite of the compromised treatment offered.

At my institute, a patient could be listed as 'poor-free' on production of the *Below Poverty-Line* card issued by the government or on certification by the head of a department. The system was helpful for a large segment of deserving, indigent patients even though there were some who were accustomed to cheat to avail of free or subsidized treatments. In the absence of an insurance cover for treatment sought outside the government hospitals, the urge to get the tests and the treatment done free at the Institute had been strong. Many managed BPL cards through wrong information or false documentation. It had been extremely difficult to filter such examples. Whether this cheating helped an individual, was entirely a matter of conscience. We were concerned more with medical aspects of management.

We all know that misery of an illness gets compounded several folds by the presence of poverty. Poverty not only tests but often humbles the powers of medicine. Looking after the poor is stressful for the practitioners of modern medicine. Most poor patients suffer from multiple problems. Moreover, the poor are generally illiterate, therefore unable to understand the complexities of diseases and their treatments. Paradoxically, the poor serve as a great source of inspiration and learning for the physicians. I remember some of those instances when the innocent comments of such patients had bowled me over. Doctor-patient dialogue in those situations becomes interesting, and sometimes even provides comic relief.

Ruldu Ram was one of my patients who would come every few months with one or more episodes of excessive bleeding from his lungs. He was a rickshaw-puller who had suffered from tuberculosis in the past. He was prescribed anti-tubercular treatment which he took for a few weeks. He stopped his treatment once he felt better. He could not afford to purchase the drugs to continue his treatment for the standard period. The Revised National Program for control of tuberculosis which provides free treatment for the disease was not in operation at that time. Thereafter, he repeatedly took medicine for short periods of a few days (or a few weeks) every time the problem re-visited. He had received several different drugs in different dosages for variable periods of time. As a result, he had developed multi-drug resistant tuberculosis along with significant lung destruction. Such a history was quite common but evoked angry response from me every time.

"You have self-destroyed yourself. There is very little I can do for you now" I told him with anger and frustration. "I am sorry sir. I have made many mistakes in the past but now I wish to make amends. I shall now complete the treatment" he replied. Before I could speak, he added: "I have brought the blood I vomited out today. I request you sir to transfuse it back to me? My children will bless you for your kind act". He was sincere when he said so. The blood he had coughed out was certainly massive.

I was stumped by his request and did not know how to respond. I tried to gather my thoughts and replied: "Look, the vomited out blood is a waste. It cannot be used for any purpose. It is impure, contaminated. Moreover, the blood gets clotted very fast". He was not convinced: "You can do everything. The science is so advanced. Why can't this blood be purified? It can be filtered. After all, it belongs to a man. Let my family not suffer due to my foolishness!"

I could understand the futility of a continued argument on blood. My anger had suddenly disappeared. I knew of his limitations. He had at least shown some concern for his children. I also realized that part of his problem lay on my side. The health system was also to blame for the continued burden of tuberculosis. I somehow reassured Ruldu Ram before he went back and hoped that he did not bleed again.

Diseases caused by self-abuse were common among the poor. It did seem to be illogical to a young physician that a poor man would spend his money on smoking or alcohol than on food and medicine. Allah Baksh had served as a labourer in a stone-crusher throughout his life. He was unable to pay for the daily needs of his family. Yet, more than half of what he earned was spent on smoking. He came to the clinic with chronic cough and severe breathlessness.

"*Sahib!* How can I purchase the drugs with my meager income?"

"Stop smoking and use the money thus saved to pay for the drugs", I made a quick reply.

"How can I continue to work if I quit? Smoking keeps me fit. It also helps to cough out the phlegm."

"Steam inhalation is quite good to cough out phlegm. You can also use cough syrups to help" I tried to advise medical remedies.

"Sir, my bowels do not move without the usual smoke. Constipation is the root cause of all my troubles. The gas from my stomach moves to the lungs and head to make me sick." he continued with his reasoning.

I was still insistent. "Take plenty of water and salads to move your bowels. You shall soon get rid of your *bidis* to save enough money for the drugs." It was then that he made the parting shot: "Sir, the cost of a bundle of *bidis* which I smoke is not even a tenth of the cost of medicine. How will it save me much? Please help me somehow to meet the costs of my treatment".

I was caught in an uncomfortable situation. I finally managed to get him some help through the 'Poor Patient Cell' of the hospital. As his disease was advanced, the relief was negligible. I was sure that a part of his problem was attributable to his constant exposure to sand-dust which he had inhaled for years. I should have also advised him to change his occupation. I knew I could not give that advice to him. That would have implied unemployment. In the absence of appropriate compensation, a loss of job would have been ruinous for him and his family.

Slowly I realized that patients' explanations of their diseases were quite amazing at times. I can recall several instances when I found myself speechless. Allah Baksh of course was logical in his reasoning. I was awestruck with Gyassudin who like Ruldu Ram was simple-minded. His argument too would seem convincing at least on surface. His case-history was presented to me at a bed-side clinic by one of the postgraduate students in medicine. He was a labourer who looked after the cattle at the farm of his employer. He had suffered from chest pain and breathlessness and was detected to have abnormal fluid in the pleural membranes covering the lungs.

Narrating the history, the medical resident informed that a milky whitish fluid was aspirated from his pleural cavity about a week ago. It was common to use vernacular terms from local languages in bed-side classes. The milky-white expression caught the immediate attention of Gyassudin who interrupted: "No Sir! It was the milk which I drank while milking the cows at the farm". I knew that the milky fluid was actually *chyle*. The resident was not at all amused. He was well informed of the nature of fluid but had not encountered such a case in the past. It was relatively uncommon to find *chyle* in the pleural cavity. The resident gave a counter explanation: "Sir, the fluid was aspirated from the pleural cavity, not the stomach". "Then this must have leaked into the lungs" Gyassudin reasoned. I had to interrupt the resident before he entered into an endless discussion. It was not easy to convince Gyasuddin. Whatever be the true cause of *chylothorax*, it constituted an exciting sight for medical residents. It was also puzzling for an ordinary patient except for milk-men like Gyassudin.

Patients frequently provide their own interpretations with incomprehensible expressions for problems which they face. Some of the concepts on lay treatments are even more interesting than the theories on causes of diseases. 'Gas from abdomen ascending to the brain' is a frequent cause of headache rooted in the Indian psyche. Similarly, 'the milk and curds being coughed out as phlegm from the lungs' is another important belief. Many such explanations are medically illogical, therefore amusing for young doctors and students. I think that such an interpretation can never be considered as a sign of illiteracy or poor understanding. Medical doctors may appear equally at odds with engineering or more precisely with social terminology.

During my under graduate years, I had heard several unbelievable stories about patients from my senior friends. Some of those tales could perhaps be fictitious jokes, but others were very close to the reality which we faced in the wards. There was a story about an old cobbler who over a period of a few days was repeatedly examined *per-rectally* for his *prostatic enlargement.* The patient was very co-operative so never refused any examination. He firmly believed that examination was an essential method of his treatment. One day, he told the Professor during the ward rounds: "Sir, I have got enough of massage for my urinary problem. Can you please discharge me now? I shall continue to administer myself the same treatment at my home".

15.

PERSEVERANCE

Bobby was a 24-year old boy who lived in a small town named Rajpura, near Chandigarh. He belonged to a well-to-do business family of that city. He used to accompany his grandfather during his visits to the hospital. The old man suffered from disabling *emphysema* with marked breathlessness. Various drugs and their combinations which different doctors used to prescribe had proved futile. He was almost bound to the wheel-chair. At that stage he needed pulmonary rehabilitation with supervised, graduated exercises and continuous use of oxygen for a better quality of life. He had kept an oxygen-cylinder at home which he used whenever he felt severely breathless. Oxygen was the only thing which helped him to some extent, at least temporarily. But he did not wish to remain tied to a cylinder. He was quite desperate and wanted to somehow get rid of his condition.

The lad was greatly attached to his grandfather. He did not accept the fact that they had reached at the end of the tunnel as far as medical treatment was concerned. He was always curious to explore other options. "There must be newer advancements in treatment", he would repeatedly ask.

Though he was a computer savvy individual, often remaining glued to his laptop surfing various sites on the internet in search of newer drugs, there was nothing substantive in what he searched. Most of the information which he brought from *Wikipedia* was common knowledge. I always felt sorry for my inability to agree with his suggestions since many a clip which he showed was promotional advertisements of obscure medicine. The rest was either gossip or occasionally some news about an *experimental drug for the future.*

Recently, he had developed a passion for television discourses which promoted aerobic exercises for healthy well-being. The T.V. programs made highly exaggerated claims that aerobic exercises could cure incurable diseases. Even cancers were reported to vanish following attendance at treatment sessions. He was convinced of the miraculous effects of physical exercises. "Exercise is a good form of natural treatment", he thought. He chose to bring the subject to my notice.

"Why not try aerobic exercises for grandpa? The breathing difficulty should be simpler to treat than a cancer." The idea caught his imagination. He desperately wanted my endorsement particularly to ensure support of his other family members. I tried to reason with him that excessive exercises could well be harmful for a sick old man. Vigorous exercises were good to promote health as well as reduce mental stress in a healthy individual. Graduated exercise constituted an important part of treatment. Though some form of exercise was essential in the presence of a stable chronic disease, an advanced disease required a very cautious approach. It was difficult to advocate the role of forced aerobics to treat a serious illness without the administration of known treatments. Rather than being beneficial, it could end with harmful outcomes. It could adversely affect the delicate physical condition of his grandfather. That was precisely what I told him. "Uncle, you are a bit too afraid. I shall show you the results after a few weeks"; he almost threw a challenge. He was determined to try the aerobic exercise treatment at home.

Bobby was convinced that an intensive course of few weeks would cure the trouble of his grandpa. He assured me that he would get over the logistic difficulties with help from other family members. The old man, tired of his continued sickness, was ready to do anything for a permanent cure. He was completely oblivious of the risks. Moreover, he was not in a fit state of mind to analyze the pros and cons.

I learnt later that a complex and complicated program of exercises followed our discussion on that day which defied all logic or common-sense. It almost looked like a cult-activity with forced exercises. The old man was physically manipulated to sit and stand erect repeatedly. He was made to squat in a crossed-leg position. Thereafter, he was made to lie flat on his back and then to sit on the floor. The steps were repeated at random without taking care of the patient's comforts or protests. The protocol also included passive stretching of arms against the walls to keep in position. Worse, the routine medication for relief of pains, restlessness and sleeplessness were withheld. Nasal douching and induced vomiting were undertaken two to three times a day as an essential component of the rejuvenation-therapy.

The old man could not bear all that rigmarole for long. His breathlessness worsened, and he lapsed into a state of semi-consciousness within a few days. It was obvious to others in the family that any further continuation would result in serious consequences. They initially consented with the trial but abandoned the idea as soon as they saw the disastrous results. All the experimental management was ended abruptly and original treatment restored. The patient was brought back to the hospital for intensive care management. Completely exhausted, he could hardly speak when he landed in the Hospital Emergency. Bobby was highly disappointed with the results of treatment and full of feelings of self-guilt. He visited me in private to say sorry. Though his goals were praiseworthy and correct, his approach was not just childish but almost infantile. He had immense affection for his grandfather. That alone could not justify the route he had adopted.

The patient lived for a few more months after that episode. I did not see the boy any further during the repeat follow-up visits. He was reprimanded by his father for precipitating the trouble. But was the boy the only one to blame? No. Others in the family had equally shared the responsibility. Though he had taken the initiative, everyone else had consented to the treatment. Bobby bore the brunt while others took the stand of non-participant bystanders.

I later came to know that Bobby got admission in a prestigious Institute for a graduate course in mechanical-engineering. It did seem to me that he was best suited for that kind of education. For most students of physical sciences, a human body is an absolute replica of a mechanical machine. I am therefore sure that he must have done well in his engineering career.

Open hand monument, the symbol of Chandigarh designed by Le Courbusier

The sprawling campus of PGIMER, Chandigarh - the institute where the author worked for over 40 years. (Photo clicked before the institute's Silver Jubilee Year, 1987-88. Several new blocks have been added since thereafter).

Images from the famous Rock Garden of Chandigarh consisting of sculptures made from thrown-away items and waste material. It is obvious that the ceramic cup from the PGI canteen (above) seen in a picture of early 1980's could not bear the vagaries of nature as can be seen in the picture clicked recently (below)

Author in the center with friends at a party during medical residency in early 1970s

Pictures from University of Washington, Seattle, USA during 1982-83 when the author was there for Fogarty International Fellowship.

Scenes from outskirts of author's home-town, Dhuri in early 1970s

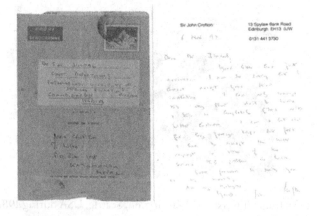

Letter from the legendary British chest physician, Sir John Crofton

Telemedicine Inauguration

Telemedicine inauguration by Sh. Manmohan Singh, Prime Minister of India (2005)

Board of Associate Editors of Chest, the international journal of cardiopulmonary diseases; author in front row (2nd from right) with Editor-in-Chief, Dr. Richard Irwin (5th from right).

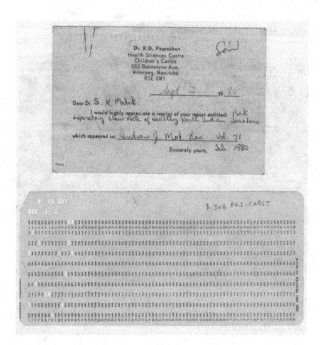

Reminders of the early period (1970s): Examples of cards used to request for reprints of articles from other authors (above), and of punch cards for feeding data into a computer (below)

First Day Cover with crossed stamp released on Ist July 2013 to commemorate the Golden Jubilee Year of the Institute

Author with Umesh, incoming Head,D. Behera, alumni and staff members of the department (30th April 2014)

16.

MR PRIME MINISTER

The message from the Ministry of External Affairs of the Government of India was crisp and clear. I was required to fly to Delhi by a scheduled flight on the same afternoon within about an hour. Though I questioned the caller repeatedly, he expressed his total ignorance. He was only supposed to convey the message of his boss, an officer in some section of the Ministry. "You shall be given details the moment you land in Delhi" I was told. He also informed that the requisite arrangements had been made and the Airlines informed about the urgency of travel. He assured me further that I would not have any problem with my travel arrangements.

It was the morning of a cloudy day in the summer. I was busy in the Outpatient Clinic with the usual rush of patients. I could understand a communication from the Health Ministry which dealt with my services. It was not uncommon to receive telephonic calls for an urgent meeting in Delhi on important issues related to health research or medical education. Occasionally, officials from the Health Ministry would seek information on subjects related to respiratory problems to frame a suitable reply to a specific question asked in Parliament. But the call from External Affairs Ministry was quite strange for me. I felt a bit tense and uneasy. My mind started to work overtime and kept going over past incidences. Had I violated a law in a foreign land during one of my earlier visits, or committed an unintended error related to a visa or the passport? Worse was the fear that someone might have mistaken me for a habitual offender or a persona non-grata. I never looked like a terrorist in any manner!

I dismissed all those possibilities after reasoning a bit. I had not travelled abroad in the last few months. It was most unlikely that a query about an external offence would be raised after a long period. But 'who knows'? It could also be possible that a VIP in the Ministry needed my professional advice. That was a soothing logic though the request for any such opinion would be made by the Director of the Institute, or rarely on a call through the Health Ministry.

Different ideas kept on reverberating in my mind. It was not long before I received another frantic call from the Institute Director's office. The issue was soon clarified. All my paranoid fears vanished into thin air. The Director informed that I ought to immediately leave for Delhi for an onward flight to a neighbouring country to attend upon her ailing Prime Minister. This was a hugely welcome relief for me. Strangely though, the earlier anxieties were replaced by a new set of worries.

I left the clinic for my home without wasting time, to collect the essential items for an over-night stay before proceeding to Chandigarh airport. The scheduled flight-time was almost due. In great haste as I was, I forgot to fetch my passport. I also missed to change my sandals for shoes on the feet. Both issues caused equal inconvenience during the visit!

I was escorted to my seat in the plane like a semi-VIP without any fuss. In Delhi, I was handed over tickets for my onward journey to Nepal. A protocol officer from the Ministry briefed me about the visit. He also gave a summary note about the arrangements in Kathmandu. The overall picture was still hazy but my mind was at ease by then. The Kathmandu flight was scheduled for mid-night. Till then, I was put up in the hostel meant for trainees of the Indian Foreign Service. That was certainly not where I thought I would be made to stay. I had expected for a comfortable hotel room to rest. For consolation however, the hostel room was fairly good in contrast to the standards of my college-hostel where I had lived as a medical resident for several years.

I faced the first test of travel at the Delhi airport when I was stopped at the Immigration counter. I did not possess an identity which would be recognized by the Immigration clerk. I knew that an Indian citizen could travel to Nepal without the mandatory requirement of a passport. I had thought that the Institute Identity Card would be an acceptable proof of residence. The immigration people wanted some more solid evidence on paper which I did not have. I had to make frantic calls to the concerned Deputy Secretary and others in the Ministry. There were a lot of cross talks between several senior officials besides my own innocent pleas. I took a big sigh of relief when the immigration officer finally relented and allowed me to travel.

I was quite apprehensive that the same problem would arise on arrival at Kathmandu airport. But as the protocol people from the Indian Embassy were there for my reception, I did not face any difficulty in entering Kathmandu. I was hurriedly escorted out of the Airport to a waiting taxi. I made a promise to myself that I would never make a fool of myself like that in the future.

I had yet to attend to my second mistake, the absence of appropriate footwear. I considered it improper to visit the Prime Minister in casual sandals. Perhaps I was a bit over conscious. I expressed my reluctance to my escort deputed by the Government of Nepal. He told me not to bother about the issue. I was not satisfied. I did not wish to project myself as an undisciplined and careless physician. I insisted on the purchase of a pair of shoes on my way to the hotel. That solved the second problem which I faced within a time span of 24 hours. It was entirely a different matter that I along with all others were required to remove our shoes at the entry of the house before we moved to the living room. It seemed that all my efforts were in vain!

Unlike in Delhi, the Kathmandu hotel was quite comfortable. I was joined by a team of local doctors including a colleague from Delhi and another from Thailand – both of whom had flown in separately. The local physician briefed all three of us with a summary of the P.M.'s medical problems and other health data. Thereafter, we were taken to the residence of our honourable patient. We did not wish to miss the chance to make a visit before he went to bed. It was already late in the evening.

The Prime Minister was immensely pleasant. He shook hands with all three of us with a smile on his face. We had already familiarized ourselves with his clinical history and investigations. I, on behalf of the team also conducted a brief but essential physical examination. The P.M. was quite cooperative and understood the necessity of some degree of physical inconvenience. He himself possessed a good medical knowledge of his problem. His personal physician too was quite intelligent. Fortunately, we all could come to a consensus conclusion without any significant disagreement. The presence of his wife helped a lot in our decision-making. There were some concerns raised by the family and the local doctors with reference to the possible side effects of drugs. We impressed upon the need of treatment and stood our ground very well. I have always believed very strongly that the patient is an active partner in decision making and disease management who also needs to accept the problems of treatment he opts to adopt.

A lot of discussion was, of course required. It all went very well. It was the PM's turn once we finished with medical explanations. He told us a lot about his visits and impressions of India. Incidentally, he had visited Chandigarh in the past when he did not have the current position of a Prime Minister. He also mentioned that his visit would have passed off as fairly ordinary but for the unexpected interference by the then Prime Minister of India who somehow came to know of his presence in Chandigarh. The Indian Prime Minister passed instructions to local officials that the visitor from Nepal should be accorded the status of a State-guest. As a result his plan to roam around the central city plaza in Sector 17 was abandoned. With a smile and some amount of resentment, he told us that he lost the freedom of an ordinary visitor.

Though he had heard about our Institute, he never had a chance to visit the place. He also talked about general health issues, the practice of medicine and the quality of doctors. There was no discussion on any issue related to the political scene either in India or Nepal. Most of the time, we listened to his discourse. It was an interesting experience and we all enjoyed the meeting. Before we left, he gave us an invitation to join him for breakfast.

The final meeting with the PM the next day at breakfast was more relaxing. A lavish spread had been laid out. In particular, I enjoyed the vegetarian menu which had been specially prepared for me. His wife was a perfect host who took personal interest in serving the dishes. We all were greatly influenced by their modesty and simplicity. I asked for his permission to click a few photographs for which he graciously agreed. For no apparent reason, his wife excused herself from the photo session. I could not ascertain the exact cause of her opting out. She was either shy or inhibited due to local traditions. It would have been highly immodest of us to dig deeper.

I along with my Indian colleague also had a meeting with a senior official of the Indian Embassy. He had a lot of questions to ask on the PM's health. We did provide a few clarifications within the limits of our professional confidentiality. He was inquisitive but did seem largely satisfied with our answers. He made me rather nervous when he casually mentioned we might have to make more visits in the future. One such visit was good and enjoyable; repeated travel would have been stressful. I was glad that there was no such requirement.

We took leave with a great degree of satisfaction. I had a glimpse of some of the important sites of Kathmandu before departing for India. A visit to the *Living Hindu Goddess* left an ever lasting impression on my mind. As per the Nepalese Hindu and Budhist traditions, a young pre-pubescent girl is designated with status of a living goddess or a Kumari and worshipped as a deity. She is venerated as an incarnation of *Chandi or Goddess Durga* who represents the might to protect the Kingdom from all evils and enemies. Of several *Kumaris* in different cities of Nepal, the Kathmandu *Royal Kumari* occupies the most distinguished place and lives in a palace. The *Kumari* home in Kathmandu survived the severe earth-quake which recently shook Nepal while a large number of buildings in the vicinity in Durbar Hall area including the old palace were devastated. The devotees attributed the miracle to the divine powers of *Kumari*.

There are a number of controversies surrounding the continuation of the *Kumari* tradition into modern times. It is quite uncertain if the same will continue in the future as was the practice in the past.

My departure from Kathmandu went well without any hiccups. The protocol people took care to obtain the requisite clearances at the airport. I did not have any time to go to the market for any further purchases. My baggage consisted of a single hand-held brief case. I had already made full use of my new pair of shoes after I returned from the PM house. I had a quiet arrival at Delhi airport; as I was not required to report in Delhi, I straightaway made my journey back to Chandigarh.

17.

MOUNTAIN OUT OF A MOLE HILL

'Your eyes do not see what your mind does not know' is an age old dictum in medicine. I had failed to notice the importance of scalded palms in the absence of my knowledge of leprosy. Those were the early days of medical school. I was able to satisfy my hurt ego by making an exotic diagnosis a few years later when I was posted as a registrar in the Emergency department of the Institute.

Mukul was a young engineering graduate from Jammu who was wheeled into the Emergency one fine day. There were several family members and friends who accompanied the patient. They all were highly agitated. The junior resident doctor who saw him first was quite confused. The patient had a referral-slip with mention of a diagnosis of tetanus. The resident had never seen a case of tetanus. Moreover, he had not faced such a situation. There was a great hue and cry all around. Noticing a significant commotion in the ward, I moved in to save the resident from being *mauled* by the hyperactive attendants. The shouts became even louder on seeing a relatively senior doctor. I had a few grey hairs on my head even at that time. It seemed that everyone was trying to outdo others to show concern.

"Doctor, do something. The boy has tetanus! Please save him!" someone shouted.

"No. He might have been bitten by a rabid dog. We do not really know. I bet it is rabies", another opined. They all continued to bombard us with their opinions and questions.

Till then, I had not had a chance to go through the problem. I decided to be firm with the supernumerary numbers. I warned that I would examine the patient only after the crowd was reduced to one or a maximum of two attendants. Reluctantly, most of them moved out even though they kept standing near the gate where I could over hear their muted talk. "We must complain against the doctor to higher authorities," someone muttered. Another thought that doctors at that big hospital were unhelpful and insensitive. I was not really bothered by those issues as I knew that things were going to change after the treatment. I had understood the diagnosis almost at the very first sight of the patient.

There was a large bunch of papers with reports of multiple investigations along with a referral slip from a local doctor. The referral note mentioned a diagnosis of tetanus following a small injury on the toe. Panic in the family was understandable since tetanus was almost always fatal. The young man had been married only a few years earlier. The wife carried an infant son in her arms and both of them were crying incessantly.

I had seen a similar case, although of lesser severity only about a few months earlier. That had given me a bit of confidence to handle the crowd with authority.

The patient had presented with characteristic '*extra pyramidal*' features, which did not fit with the diagnosis of tetanus. Sudden appearance of such a group of symptoms and signs occasionally follow the administration of drugs used for nausea and vomiting. I got a confirmatory reply to my very first question on the use of such a drug. He had been given an injection of an *anti-emetic* drug for persistent vomiting after consuming uncooked, street food. Within an hour, bizarre manifestations appeared which confused the local doctors. It was difficult to diagnose a problem which perhaps they had not confronted in the past. Tetanus on the other hand was a more familiar illness.

Commonly known as '*lock-jaw*', tetanus is a painful condition characterized by an extreme degree of rigidity of muscles, clenching of teeth and convulsions. Separate wards for tetanus were maintained in several hospitals. A nationwide use of anti-tetanus vaccine and sterilization measures has brought tetanus almost to the brink of disappearance. Mukul had shown some features mimicking tetanus in the form of stiff muscles, abnormal movements of the head and arms, facial grimacing, inability to open the mouth and to reply to questions.

Recovery following the treatment was quite dramatic. He was up and about by the evening. He smiled when I went to see him in the evening. The family was relieved of the tension which had built-up in the last few days and were laughing and talking. One of the members, perhaps the father did express thanks. But no one else bothered to utter even a single word of remorse for the rude behaviour with the staff. It seemed as if nothing significant was done by the team. Perhaps a drama should have been created with administration of multiple injections, intravenous drips, oxygen cylinders and other interventions. A single injection was too simple a treatment to acknowledge. This was a kind of enigma which I learned over time. Slowly, it becomes a part of my professional life.

The picture continued to flash in front of my eyes for several weeks. Even today, I can visualize that scene of wailing and hysterical people tinged now with a sense of satisfaction and pride. I have frequently cited the case to my students as an example when a seemingly serious or big diagnosis may in fact be quite innocuous. It may finally prove to be a *mountain made out of a mole-hill*. Not infrequently, such an example becomes a source of embarrassment for the doctor who had initially diagnosed the illness. Often, this happens because of the rarity of occurrence of the problem. Medical literature is replete with such case-reports of unusual or odd manifestations.

It was about a quarter of century later that my son Aditya, himself a doctor narrated a similar story to me, although entirely in a different context for a different problem. After completion of his medical internship, he happened to take a skiing trip to the *Garhwal* Mountains in the Himalayas to get rid of the tension of post-graduation entrance examination. He, along with a cousin proceeded on a few days' leave. I narrate the incidence below in his own words which he had reported later in his college Newsletter of Sir Ganga Ram Hospital, New Delhi.

"We went to Auli, a hamlet situated 12 km uphill of Joshimath, on the great pilgrim route to Badrinath. The snow clad hills and the fresh air were liberating. After being fitted out with the skiing gear we hit the slopes, all too literally. It was a beginners' course and the first thing which was taught was

how to fall. One of the instructors even boasted that he knew of fifty ways to fall!

Soon, one fact emerged – I was the only doctor for miles around. My nascent ability was soon put to the test when I received a message one fine morning while I was out skiing, requesting me to attend to a young British lady who had taken a tumble somewhere on the slopes. The history was that of falling on her right hand. As I went to see her, the morbid thoughts of Colles' fractures and elbow dislocations were hammering inside my head, not to mention the butterflies fluttering in my stomach. Though I had done a lot of hard work during my internship, this was to be my first taste of independent decision making; never had I felt the need of a senior so badly.

Anyway, on examining her, all I found was an area of pain and tenderness localized over the base of the right thumb. I had seen a small clinic in Joshimath when we had arrived, so I sent her there to get an x-ray done after prescribing some pain killers, of which they had an ample stock, already! Later, we met at dinner that day and I was solemnly informed that the x-ray showed a fracture. Both of them were very worried and planned to cut short the trip to go back for proper treatment. I myself felt sorry for them but could not help. Casually. I asked to see the x-ray. The moment I saw the x-ray I burst out laughing, for the 'fracture' was nothing more than a smooth round 'sesamoid bone' lying lateral to the head of the first metacarpal bone!

I explained this to the couple and told them nothing more needed to be done. A 'sesamoid' is a small piece of an accessory bone, sometimes found in the attachment of, but separately from a normal bone. They both were quite assured and understood the problem. I returned home soon after, after refusing payment from the grateful couple, feeling refreshed and with a renewed belief in the medical profession".

I am sure that the Briton accompanied by her friend must have spent the rest of their holidays gleefully. It is not possible to say what both the tourists back home, thought about those instances. They must have talked of their wonderful experience in the hills.

Individually, we had gained confidence from those incidents. Aditya had joyfully learnt a lesson. His rejuvenated interest after the trip had helped him not only in learning but doing more. One should consider oneself fortunate to acquire the power of practical knowledge in the early part of one's careers. Such an experience I believe is a valuable asset which a doctor would wish to possess.

A more recent incident was told to me by my daughter Manishi who is also a doctor. She had a woman in her clinic who had delivered a healthy baby in the evening. There was no problem with the mother and the baby when they went to sleep. However, early in the morning, all hell broke loose. The duty nurse noticed a dusky hue over the face of the mother. The bluish tinged skin was rightly considered a sign of *'cyanosis'* implying lack of oxygen in the body. *Cyanosis* is a serious condition which sometimes necessitates the need for assisted respiration with a mechanical ventilator. The doctors feared a serious complication. However, the woman was comfortable. Moreover, the oxygen saturation was normal. Yet they considered it wise to administer oxygen and ask for a medical consultation. The anesthetist on duty was also informed.

The patient had quietly noticed frantic activities going on around her. She kept on enjoying the increased attention being given to her. Finally she inquired about the reason of all the hustle and bustle. When told of the presence of bluish hue, the patient volunteered an explanation: "That must be the colour of my *dupatta*". Truly so! She wore a blue shawl which had leaked colour on to her face. The spurious *cyanosis* was easily wiped off with a wet cloth. The entire medical team heaved a sigh of relief. They were happy even though they had to cut a sorry figure. Presence of true *cyanosis* would have been worse and more troublesome for all concerned.

18.

CORPORATE HONCHOS

Mr. Rai was a corporate manager who controlled a large number of commercial establishments of a big business house in different parts of India. He had also accumulated a large personal wealth through investments in shares and debentures of different companies. It was a classical story of rags to riches. "I did not win a lottery worth millions. I had to put my heart and soul into my work to reach this stage", he often said with pride. He had come to see me for the first time for a late after-noon meeting after a specific request was made by his secretary.

Prima facie, there was nothing unusual. Requests for special consultations for some prominent people were routinely received by many of us at the Institute. However, the request for Mr. Rai was somewhat different from other routine requests since he wanted to be seen alone. He had requested for a late after-noon meeting in the absence of any other individual or assistant. Somewhat perplexed, I acceded. Most of the times, patients were accompanied by more than one attendant. I had no problem with the patient being alone. In any case, it was always a time-consuming and difficult task to satisfy multiple attendants of patients.

A meeting with only the patient was more welcome, as it was likely to be quiet and short.

It was a typical lazy winter afternoon. Mr. Rai was a stocky individual of a pleasant nature. Like Sumer Singh (of Pickwick Papers), Rai had the troublesome problem of excessive snoring and sleepiness. He frequently used to doze off during work, even while attending the meetings with administrative and government officials. His staff members had to frequently repeat their briefings. Many of them would make a mockery of his behaviour at his back. Mr. Rai was often embarrassed and had to offer one or the other explanation. He would commonly attribute the sleepiness to a late night function, headache or some other similar problem. Almost everyone in the office was aware of his lame excuses. Even his family despaired of his habit.

As the problem was fast getting worse, he had hesitatingly agreed to suggestions by friends and well-wishers to visit the hospital. It was not an easy decision for him. He could not gather courage to do so openly, considering it necessary to hide the fact from others in his staff. It has been my consistent observation that while patients gloat over the presence of a chronic heart ailment and even boast of high blood pressure or blood sugar levels, the diagnosis of a sleep and snoring problem is considered a stigma. Likewise, Mr. Rai did not wish to become a laughing stock in front of others. At least that is what he thought was likely to happen.

Mr. Rai's arrival was apparently without any information in his office, but I am sure that at least some of his staff members were aware of his visit. It was unnecessary on my part to poke into the issue. After the initial pleasantries, I asked him about his problem. He was rather evasive, tried to trivialize – "I do not have any problem, it is just an occasional cough which bothers people at the office".

"Do you bring out phlegm, along with your cough?"

"No, it is rather very rare and scanty, does not disturb my work schedule".

"Any breathlessness, restlessness or change in weight ….?" I kept on listing the symptoms and coaxing him to come out with history.

"Do you snore excessively during your sleep?" Finally I chose to be direct in my questioning.

"Yes, I do", he admitted with a degree of reluctance, "It is my wife who often tells me so".

"Do you feel sleepy during the day?"

"Yes, sometimes. More so when I am tired", He replied.

Once he had opened up, he continued and narrated the full story without hesitation. I only had to make occasional interjections here and there.

I patiently listened to him. Perhaps it was the first time ever that he was liberal with details. He admitted that he always wanted to seek help but felt inhibited.

"Please keep it all to yourself. I do not wish to be seen as sick or dependent." He finally ended his tale of misery. I assured him of utmost confidentiality which doctors observe in treatment of patients. "Of course you need to make a repeat visit for purpose of investigations." I told him with a degree of firmness. With great reluctance and reservation, he agreed to go through the 'cumbersome set of tests'.

The diagnosis was fairly obvious and adequately documented after the sleep study. The treatment involved the application of pressured air during sleep delivered with the help of a small ventilator. It required the regular use of a tight-fitting mask over the nose and the mouth. The pressure was essential to prevent the collapse of the upper air-passages which happened during sleep. The suggestion did not go well with Mr. Rai. It was not very pleasant to be tied daily to a machine, certainly not for a person like Mr. Rai.

"Why can't you try some medicine first? I am sure that a simpler management is going to be a better option".

"It certainly is. But drugs don't help this problem. We shall unnecessarily waste time if we choose that path. Of course, you need to shed weight. The earlier you opt for treatment, the better you shall feel", I tried to argue with him.

In spite of all the reasoning I could put forward, it took several months before Mr. Rai decided to go for the recommended method of treatment. In all probabilities, the decision was preceded by an internet search for other possible treatments compounded by failure of prescriptions by different physicians who must have complied with his wishes.

When he finally chose to go in for the prescribed management, it worked remarkably well. He was a changed man. The very next day, his wife confided in me that she had slept comfortably at night, almost for the first time since after her marriage. Jocularly she said that her husband's snoring at night sometimes exceeded the sound of a moving train at full speed. That reminded me of another wife who had compared the sound with that of an aeroplane landing. Though the poor-soul was the real victim in this case, she hardly ever complained!

The change in behaviour of Mr. Rai was noticeable. He lost weight and looked fitter after the treatment. He was also more alert and attentive in his office. That did ruffle the hair of a few notorious staff members who were habitual late comers. None of those changes mattered for Mr. Rai. He continued to pretend that he did not have any health issue in the past and wished to seek an alternate treatment.

At each visit, Mr. Rai would indulge in an informal discourse. But for his views on his illness, he was quite upright on debatable issues. Unlike many a business manager, he would not bother to hide his opinion. It was interesting to listen to him on the subject of ethics in business. "It is surprising to find that nothing moves these days without greasing the palms of officials. Everybody is interested in making easy money." He was rather upset at the increasing trend of corruption in every field. "What can we do? We cannot remain in business without paying for requisite licenses and other approvals." He would not even listen to a suggestion to complain to a higher authority. "The rot is there up to the top. It is better to keep quiet. We are interested in running the business smoothly. No one in the company board is ready to listen to excuses" he would often surmise. "Ethics? Ethics are important only if practiced in reciprocity. We cannot preach ethical standards in isolation. Even the judiciary is not free from corrupt practices".

I always hesitated in entering into a non-professional discussion. Mostly, I would listen to than agree with his opinion or express my own views and suggestions.

Why Mr. Rai initially landed himself in an awkward situation, was quite enigmatic. It seems that some patients are mortally afraid of adversity. They tend to deny the very existence of a problem. A denial for a short time is often a good coping mechanism. Continued denial however, is dangerous and allows the underlying problem to become monstrous. There is the famous analogy of the pigeon and cat story. The pigeon closes its eyes to shut out the sight of a cat; but the danger continues to lurk and the cat finally catches the pigeon.

Mr. Kapoor was another well-placed but highly anxious businessman. He was excessively inquisitive about his health but poor in following the treatment. He would listen to all what I had to say but conveniently forget all advice the moment he left my office. It was difficult to satisfactorily reply to the clarifications which he often sought. He used to go into minute details of inquiring into the exact hours and minutes of drug administration, whether before or after the meals, whether with water, tea or milk. Worse, he would ask about each edible item which he could consume -whether he could eat a banana, a potato, rice, papaya or an onion. Although relevant, the questions were rather repetitive. The questioning often tested my patience making me edgy. Somehow I successfully avoided showing my annoyance.

I was put in a particularly embarrassing situation one night at a party hosted by a common friend, Raghuvir. Like most other Punjabi hosts, he was keen that Mr. Kapoor should toast a drink. "One or two drinks are not going to cause any harm. You can ask Dr. Jindal who will also agree with the idea", Raghuvir tried to put weight to his invitation. To justify his possible indiscretion with diet, Kapoor was insistent that I should give a nod before the drinks. I did not wish to become a scapegoat in that situation. The argument went on and on until a senior lawyer at the party intervened.

He somehow convinced Mr. Kapoor to share a drink to the satisfaction of the host. It also seemed tempting for Mr. Kapoor to find an excuse for his drinks.

Rai and Kapoor had achieved pinnacles of success in their business enterprises. But both were indiscreet in their attitudes towards management of disease. I am often bothered to notice the presence of dichotomous behaviour in people who are otherwise uncompromising. Though they have been top achievers in their profession work, their health practices are almost opposite to their rules of business management. 'Why it is so?' has remained an unanswered question in my mind.

19.

'IF A MAN'S LUNGS PANT WITH HIS WORK'

It was during the early hours of dawn when I was aroused by the constant ringing of the telephone at my residence. This was an urgent call from the son of a civil court judge, Mr. Sharma who had recently moved to the city. Mr. Sharma desperately needed my help for a serious attack of breathlessness. The family had waited for some time with treatment at home before deciding to call for help. He lived in a government house in a neighbouring sector of the city, not far from my own house. I would have preferred for him to reach the hospital Emergency for immediate management but his son was already at my doors.

I reached his house within a few minutes. He was finding it difficult to breathe. It was still considered wise to get him to the hospital for a few days. With some initial aid, it became possible to stabilize him before he was transported. It was the availability of quality medical assistance at his home that saved him from serious consequences. He had history of similar attacks in the past. I was also informed that he was quite erratic with his maintenance treatment. That was the major cause of concern for the family. They had therefore adequate arrangements at home to avoid a bad situation.

In the case of the present episode, Mr. Sharma improved and was discharged after a few days. He went back to his work, but his behaviour remained unchanged. He was in a particularly jovial mood when he visited me next for follow-up advice. He was grateful for all that had been done to save his life but remained evasive about his compliance with treatment. Rather than speaking about himself, he started with his suggestions to improve the functioning of the hospital. He seemed to have noticed several deficiencies in the wards which he did not hesitate to point out.

Mr. Sharma was particularly concerned that the poor and the 'common' people might not receive the same benefits of treatment which he did as a more privileged person. I repeatedly tried to cut him short to talk about his follow-up treatment – "Mr. Sharma you must tell me the current medication you are using. Are you now able to carry on with your daily activities?" My questions hardly registered with him. He carried on his monologue, as always in the past. Finally, he left after thanking me for my advice without ever listening to what I had to say. I felt rather annoyed and defeated.

Mr. Sharma's attitude towards his illness was unexpectedly illogical for an otherwise reasonable man. He was very poor in following medical instructions. He would frequently self-medicate, sometimes ignore and at other times over-use his drugs. Not infrequently, his daily dose of drugs would be more than double the prescribed dosages. He would not hesitate to keep on increasing the number of inhaled puffs at the slightest presence of cough.

In terms of doctors' jargon, he qualified as a 'bad-patient'. That factor was significantly responsible for the poor control of his asthma.

His treatment policy was also affected because of the advice given by ill-informed doctors and friends. Medical advice is sometimes diluted to comply with the wishes or dictates of important patients. The option of acceptance of a particular treatment is certainly a patient's right. But he/she must be made aware of the disadvantages or futility of a sub-optimal treatment. Succumbing to pressure invariably works adversely for the patient's interests.

As long as he remained at Chandigarh, Mr. Sharma kept on inquiring about discovery of newer drugs for his illness. "Why is it so difficult to discover a curative treatment for this allergy? So much progress is happening in medical science every day." Sometimes it seemed that I was personally responsible for the lack of medicinal treatment of his problem. I was however helpless in the matter.

After about a year, Mr. Sharma was transferred out of Chandigarh. A few days before he moved out, he invited me to his home for dinner. No other guest was invited to join. "Dr. Jindal, you may not appreciate how thankful I have been for all your care. I do feel remarkably better in spite of the fact that I do not like the treatment." It was perhaps the first time he accepted feeling better.

Asthma of variable severity is common but the choking type is highly enigmatic. Such an acute attack of asthma can be as dramatic as a fit of epilepsy. This enigmatic presentation as *"If a man's lungs pant with his work"* described in the Babylonian "Code of Hammurabi" however remains the most ancient form of asthma known from almost two millennia

BC. Hippocrates the father of Medicine who was the first to use the term "Asthma" also defined the disease in similar terms- *panting* and *respiratory distress*. It is always frightening to notice an apparently healthy individual worsening rapidly and finding it hard to breathe. President Theodore Roosevelt is said to have suffered from terrifying night-time smothering attacks during his childhood in the 19th century. There was no effective treatment for asthma at that time.

The family members of Mr. Sharma were fairly brave to tackle the situation. They had adequately equipped the house with drugs and devices including an oxygen cylinder in case of an emergency situation, like the one they had faced on that day. One had to be extremely cautious for such patients with unstable presentations. Patients with brittle manifestations which physicians sometime refer to as 'near-fatal asthma' hardly give any time before they land in serious, sometime fatal complications. Only an immediate intervention can save one's life.

Incidentally, Justice Chaturvedi also suffered from similar episodes of sudden breathlessness, panting and cough. Although regular in his treatment-schedule, Justice Chaturvedi had a passion for alternate treatments besides his inhalers. He had experimented with acupuncture treatment as well as yoga sessions in the past. He had also tried some magical water from a 'miracle spring' in Himachal Pradesh famous for its curative value. Each time, he felt an additional relief which did not last long. But he remained on one or the other herbal drug all the time.

Justice Chaturvedi was a simple but talkative individual. It was highly unusual for a person in a high chair to act as unassumingly as he would. But Justice Chaturvedi enjoyed his individuality. He did not shy away from the fact that he suffered from a condition which made him seek frequent medical consultations. He would personally call for an appointment, observe punctuality and always arrive in time. "Not keeping with time is disrespect for the person with whom you plan to meet". I started liking him for his diligence.

After failing to find a permanent relief, Justice Chaturvedi settled for his current therapy for some time. But the satisfaction did not last for long. He came back to inquire about my experience with and 'permission' for 'fish-treatment' for his asthma. That was highly unusual considering my area of work. I had known of the practice through several news reports in the media. I had also seen a few patients who had gone through one or more treatment sessions. None of them could claim a permanent cure. In the absence of any scientific data to support the claim, I found it extremely difficult to offer an affirmative opinion to Justice Chaturvedi which he had expected from me.

"If you strongly believe that the treatment could help, you can surely try", I left the choice to his personal decision.

"But I am a vegetarian. I have never consumed a fish, that too a live fish! It is quite repelling for me" he said with some degree of disappointment.

"They administer the drug mixed in *jaggery* for vegetarians. But it is supposed to take a longer time to give some relief", I told him as read in news-report. He was not satisfied. I later learnt that he did not pursue fish-treatment. Apparently, he continued to do fairly well with his inhalational treatment and other herbal drugs.

Miracle fish-therapy continues to be practiced by Bathini brothers of Goud family of Hyderabad. A live sardine fish with a yellow herbal medicine in its mouth is directly slipped into the throat of a patient by a Goud brother on the specific day/s of *Mrigasira Karti* which marks the onset of monsoon according to Hindu calendar. Several thousands of people gather in the city for treatment on that most auspicious day. Widespread arrangements are made for free camping and food by social organizations and the local administration for the people coming to seek treatment. It has happened occasionally that the fish is slipped into the larynx resulting in violent cough and breathlessness.

Asthma treatment continues to baffle patients and clinicians alike. A large number of complementary therapies are available in different parts of the world. In addition to the Allopathic drugs including the inhalers, various kinds of Ayurvedic, Unani and Homeopathic medicine are widely used. Yoga therapy remains a widely practiced ancient Indian method for the treatment. Natural therapies with diet, exercise, and life-style modifications, massage, nutritional supplementation, hypnosis, art and music are also advocated by different practitioners.

Other remedies include the traditional Chinese herbs, acupuncture, osteopathy and Chiropractice. Not commonly practiced in India, Buteyko, a form of nasal breathing and breath-control is in vogue in some parts of Eastern Europe. The technique was popularized in Russia in the 1950s by an Ukranian doctor who had hypothesized increased respiratory rate as the cause of asthma. There are strong support groups for each form of treatment. To me, it seems that some of these methods provide additional benefit especially to people who believe in the same; but the modern inhalational therapy remains the corner-stone of treatment.

20.

ERYTHROCYTE SEDIMENTATION RATE

Sarup Kaur was an elderly lady in her eighties who had none from her family in the city to look after her. She was tired of the long journey of life. She would invariably describe her life as 'a bit of bore' during her visits. Fortunately, she had enough money to enjoy the comforts of her physical possessions. Her two sons were settled abroad. They never hesitated to send her money but found it difficult to come for a long visit. Her husband had died some years ago. The old soul suffered from loneliness and isolation in a large one thousand square yard bungalow, located in a posh sector of Chandigarh. She had persistently refused to go to America to live with her sons. She often complained, "America is not a country for an old woman like me to live. Everyone there is busy in his or her life."

"But you have your sons and their families to take care of you and keep you busy", I tried to impress upon the merits of going there and living with the children.

"My sons do not find time to talk to me. I cannot commute on my own. It is difficult for me to communicate with the grand-children. I hardly understand the way they speak. They speak fast with a twisted tongue". She was rather bitter in her expression, "A poor creature like me is more of a burden. My daughters-in-law do not respect me the way they do in India. Sometime, I do not find the chance to utter a single word throughout the day". She further added: "After the loss of my husband Mohinder, I prefer to spend the rest of my life here in India. I have Bahadur as my domestic help and a maid named Ranjeeto with me to take care of my personal needs." Bahadur was a loyal attendant who invariably accompanied the old woman during all her visits.

Sarup Kaur got addicted to the hospital after she suffered from a genuine episode of pneumonia. Although she recovered from her illness after a brief hospitalization, she maintained the regularity of hospital visits with one or the other pretext. Finally, she decided in favour of an abnormal *erythrocyte sedimentation rate*, popularly referred to as ESR as the preferential excuse. The importance of high ESR was impressed upon her by an enlightened friend with whom she used to share gossip every evening in the nearby garden. Soon she was duly informed of a large number of possible causes of high ESR making it easy for her to choose one every visit.

The possibility of an occult cancer was the most attractive pick. "I am not worried about death, but please tell me how much time is left for me", was her standard question at each visit. Invariably, it made my task difficult in relieving her fears. I had to find long winding explanations to answer her questions. She also underwent through an unending battery of investigations including the PET scanning and an arduous gastrointestinal endoscopy. A number of medical practitioners happily complied with her wishes.

Sarup Kaur repeatedly narrated the same story every time she visited the Clinic. I must also admit of my inability to lower the *ESR* in spite of my best efforts spread over almost a decade in her case. Yet she possessed a great degree of faith. She would never hesitate to shower praise for my treatment and bless me with a long life. It was me who felt failure. All my efforts to refer her to other physicians or to other hospitals did not bear any fruit.

ESR continued to bother me and my staff for several years. Sarup Kaur remained a crusader patient. Importantly, she was never in a hurry. She found the waiting room quite a convenient place to spend time where she was able to enjoy the company of other patients and share stories. I had meanwhile learnt that ESR was possibly an ideal excuse for the outing for a lonely senior as much as for young house-wives who found it difficult to keep busy in kitty parties. Who can prove a better target than a doctor? A doctor needs to listen to your symptoms with patience even if he comes to realize the real motive. Howsoever superficial or repetitive it might be, the fear expressed by a patient could prove to be true.

The astute British clinician, Dr. Richard Asher had aptly described the reason of a patient to repeatedly talk to a physician: "To lonely people, a medical consultation may represent an event of great importance. It supplies that need to be noticed that exists in all human beings. A patient may be too proud to complain of loneliness, but there is no loss of pride in complaining of symptoms".

Aman's visits to the Chest Clinic were as regular and as frequent as those of Sarup Kaur. Both of them had diametrically opposite personalities and backgrounds. Aman was a young man in his mid-thirties who always bubbled with enthusiasm. He possessed a strong will to remain fit and regularly visited a Gym. His wealthy in-laws in the city were seriously concerned about his illness. Constantly worried about his health, his wife Radha or someone else from the family accompanied him at every visit. Aman and Radha had no child of their own and spent a lot of their time in social and charitable activities.

Aman had first reported with symptoms of cold and cough to a family-physician who practiced in his neighbour-hood. On routine clinical investigations, a mild increase in his ESR was noticed. The physician prescribed him a number of drugs and asked for a follow-up visit after a week. He was not much bothered once he felt better after a few days. But the wife got worried by the finding of high ESR when she mentioned the problem to a friend at a kitty-party. She was advised to get an immediate advice by a specialist. The domestic help of the friend had suffered from tuberculosis in the past. "His ESR was also raised" she told Radha.

Once informed, Aman got equally concerned. His physician promptly obliged in referring him to the Chest Clinic of the Institute. On recommendation of a common friend, he was seen by me in the hospital. That was the beginning of a regular expenditure of ten to fifteen minutes of my busy outpatient time in the hospital. Incidentally, there were no costs at the Institute for the outpatient consultations. I am sure that the crowd of patients waiting for their turns would have been cursing me for this indiscretion with time. We used to have around 300 or more patients, to be seen and advised on every clinic-day in a time span of a few hours. Each one of the consultants in the Clinic had only about five minute for each patient, on an average. The time distribution always went astray. It is true that each patient needed more time than what we could afford. Some patients like Aman, needed even more.

Radha was quite verbal in citing the problems of her husband. "Doctor, please have a careful look at his test. Does he suffer from tuberculosis? His ESR is high. My friend has advised me to see you for thorough investigations."

The abnormality seemed unimportant to me but I did not wish to take a chance. I ran him through a chest X-ray and other essential tests. Everything was quite normal. I assured both of them and told them not to worry about tuberculosis in view of the normal test reports. Moreover, he did not have any symptom worth a mention. Apparently convinced, they went back home. I felt a bit relieved after the tiresome interview which seemed almost similar to the one for my selection for the faculty of the Institute.

Lo and behold, he came back after a few weeks accompanied by his over-expressive wife and mother-in-law. He was suffering from the same complaint of 'still high ESR'. Most of the questions were repeated verbatim. The only difference being the additional barbs by the mother-in-law. She was far more inquisitive than her daughter and son-in-law. These interviews continued almost endlessly. His ESR was almost normal. It did not bother me as a doctor; I was not even sure about the genuineness of reports. But I must also admit that the whole family was highly courteous. They would pay profuse thanks at each visit. I could not dismiss them without a talk.

For me, there was one common link between Aman and Sarup Kaur- 'raised *ESR'* in medical parlance. ESR caught fancy largely because of the high incidence of tuberculosis for which the test was most frequently used. The test was first discovered by Edmund Biernacki, a Polish pathologist in the late 19th century, hence known as *Biernacki's Reaction* in some countries. Indian doctors commonly follow the British terminology of *Westergren test*. It remains a commonly misinterpreted blood test in this country.

Somehow, a raised ESR has become synonymous with the diagnosis of tuberculosis even though it is known to happen in a large number of non-tubercular inflammatory and other chronic diseases. There are several other simple causes of high ESR, such as an episode of common cold or the presence of anemia. ESR is spuriously high if blood for the test is obtained after a heavy meal. This in fact is a trick employed by anxious and attention seeking people to demonstrate a state of ill health. The test requires at least an hour to perform which is an important pitfall. Not infrequently, a busy laboratory technician may tend to shorten the period of observation.

21.

TEENAGE HICCUPS

"We need to get her in for appropriate treatment." I clearly told Babli's parents who had brought her to the hospital for her fever and cough. Babli had an abscess in her lung which had developed after an episode of pneumonia. Irregular and inadequate treatment at home had resulted in that complication. She required urgent admission for effective treatment.

"But uncle, I have a lot of syllabus to cover for my Board examinations. I have not yet undertaken a single revision. There is no question of my getting in the hospital. You give me some medicine to get me well." She flatly refused the advice.

"Hospitalization is necessary for injectable treatment which cannot be done at home without adequately supervised monitoring" I insisted.

"Uncle, my body keeps on burning with high fever. Moreover, I keep on coughing throughout the day. I cannot sleep well and feel very weak. How can I get admitted in that condition? Please treat me soon", she pleaded, still not convinced.

When I tried to explain she refused to listen. Angrily, she walked out of the chamber on being advised. This was a tense situation for the family who were extremely worried about her deteriorating health. The father tried to apologize for her behaviour. But that was not an issue of significance for me. I had faced such situations before. I was more concerned about the possible impact of her neglect on her condition. Babli represented the typical class of young teenagers who when sick, are unable to cope with illness. Disease is rather an alien concept at this age. She lived in her own dreams with a lot many ambitions. She wanted to become a doctor herself and did not wish to lose her chance. But she was severely threatened by her illness. She had to be helped, but how?

I could neither convince her about treatment decisions nor assure a good recovery without a satisfactory management plan. It was futile to argue about the illness. I did explain the issues to her father who was quite confused. I decided to be firm with her rather than prescribe a half-hearted treatment. I called her back to my chamber, mildly admonished and warned that she would not become a good doctor if she failed to accept a doctor's advice herself. "If you insist to go back, you may leave. Do not come back to me. You may report to the Emergency in case you get worse at night", I told her curtly. She left in a huff. I knew that she would come back. There was no alternate option. It was just not possible to continue with studies in the presence of high fever, an awful cough and sputum production. The father promised to bring her back whenever she decided to change her mind.

She returned to the out-patient clinic before it was over. On her way back home, she had a severe bout of cough, now with a mild blood tinge of the phlegm. She was completely exhausted because of constant coughing. She was almost crying, feeling like a helpless bird trapped in a cage. I just smiled while she poured out an emotional outburst on doctors and diseases. She kept on cursing herself on her fate. After a long and meaningless monologue, she again inquired from me – "What next? Now what do you want me to do?" Patiently, I told her that she would get well but needed to stay in the hospital for a few days. Her cries soon transformed to sobs. She finally agreed with a weak smile. She did extract a promise to be discharged as soon as she got well.

Her attitude during hospitalization was totally different. She obediently followed the instructions of nurses and doctors regarding her treatment. She was determined to prove a good student for study of medicine. Rightly so, she showed a remarkable recovery within the next two days. She had a broad smile on her face when told of discharge. Her symptoms had almost completely disappeared. She went back home in less than a week without missing her Board examinations. I was later told by the father that she managed to pass with satisfactory marks. They also decided to contribute to the burden of sweets in our kitty!

Handling of a sick teenager is always a trial of patience for a doctor. It requires a careful approach. Teenagers are rather sensitive individuals. They are more difficult to handle than small children. Children can often be coaxed to accept what doctors consider as fair. A teenager can neither be convinced nor bribed. Medical logic does not find a high place in his or her mind at a tender age. Babli for example, could harm herself due to her ignorance. Her father was an intelligent person who appreciated the need for urgent treatment. Not infrequently, the parents fail to understand the potential damages of negligence. Parents who get panicked even more than the sick child only add to the woes of doctors. Too much cribbing or whining does nothing more than adding to the problems of management.

Teenage reactions are not just spontaneous but can also be rebellious. Anil proved one of the most glaring examples. Anil, an only child, suffered from chronic asthma ever since his childhood. His mother had always pitied him for his bad health. She was poor at handling her son and his illness. Almost always, she would curse and cry every time she accompanied him to the Clinic. "Doctor Sir! My son has a miserable health. He keeps on coughing. He hardly sleeps at night. The whole family is disturbed because of his problem." I tried to interrupt her elaborate description of his illness which was familiar to me. She however continued: "He does not eat well. His performance in his school is quite poor. I am afraid that he might fail his examinations."

"I am sure that his condition is manageable. We need to be patient. There is no need to panic." I always tried to give some assurance.

"No. Doctor I am sure that he will never get well. It seems that we all are doomed to suffer. Blessed are the parents whose children are healthy! Do you not have a drug which can cure his illness?" She would continue with uncensored verbosity.

I could always sense a shadow of repulsion on Anil's face. He would quietly sit and listen to the conversation between the two of us. I felt bad that she would constantly single him out for his illness and poor performance. It was true that she was worried and deeply concerned. But she was quite indiscreet in her behaviour. All her talk added to the guilt which the boy had developed over the years.

The bubble suddenly burst one day when the two had come together for a follow-up visit. As soon as she began with her repetitive story, the boy started shouting. Unmindful of the crowd of other patients he shrieked: "So what? Let me fail. I do not wish to study at all." He was extremely agitated.

The mother replied without realization of his anger. "It is not honourable to fail. No one in our family has ever done so. I wish that you could do well. I do not know from where you got this illness."

That was enough to add fuel to the fire. He squarely blamed her for all his suffering. "Mother, I got the problem from you. I had never asked to be born. I should better die so as to let you live in peace", was all he could say clearly amidst his sobs. He was red and furious almost to the point of hurting her. The mother was aghast at his sudden outburst.

With great difficulty, I along with an assistant cooled him down. We took him to a side-room, offered a glass of water and let his anger die down. He continued to sob but did not say much thereafter. Meanwhile, the mother had started crying. She was now blaming her own fate. It was not at all easy to make the mother understand the problem. I also considered it more appropriate to postpone any further discussion. After a while, both went away when the initial shock was over.

I had advised her to seek counselling of a clinical psychologist. I do not know if she had heeded that advice. On my own, I could not follow it any further. They never came for a revisit.

22.

WEAKNESS OF THE POWERFUL

I had also the opportunity to look after people in high positions of power which included senior ministers, Chief Ministers and governors of states for one or the other respiratory problem at various times. The experience had been quite satisfying even though it was always like walking on a tight rope. Talking straight and truthfully with this class of patients was neither easy nor totally safe. One could end up with criticism and sometimes, Inquiries and Commissions. It was a professional risk which was always there in any distinguished company. It was always important to understand the attitude of a V.I.P. towards an illness to assess his/ her strengths and weaknesses. This had greatly helped to resolve at least some of the complex issues of treatment plans.

As always, there was many a difference between the behaviour of different V.I.Ps during treatment. One 'Governor' was so careful about drug usage that he personally maintained an impeccable record of each tablet and each inhalation of medicine in his diary. He would not tolerate a sneeze to distract his attention. He recorded his daily weight in grams to show to his physician. Another

Governor was so care free that he never bothered to know even the names of the drugs he was regularly on for years even when out of office. His daily treatment schedule was the total responsibility of the medical team attached to him. He would engulf without hesitation whatever was given to him. Whenever I went to see him he would not listen to what I had to say. "Doctor Sahib, tell these '*boys*' what I need to do" was his standard reply. The 'boys' belonging to his medical team were always on their toes.

On one occasion, a Governor of a distant state visited the Institute with complaints of breathlessness and cough. A retired senior commander of the Indian Army, the Governor possessed an overbearing personality. He hardly gave any time for others to speak. But for interruptions due to his cough, he continued to talk endlessly. With a long career spanning over a few decades, he possessed an immense, hidden treasury of tales to tell his audience. I, as usual, was a soft target. He narrated innumerable stories of different postings which he had in the past from Kashmir to Kanyakumari.

It was a real feast to enjoy the stories of courage and conviction. The only problem was the lack of patience to sit silently and listen. It was difficult for me to keep on nodding to whatever he said. I only wished to convey an opinion on the medical condition for which he had come. Somehow, that did not seem to happen. The ice was broken when an assistant knocked in to inform of some important meeting in an hour or so. I grabbed the opportunity to rapidly fire my questions on his problem.

"Sir, since when do you have this nasty cough?"

"Ever since I returned from the Hills!...." I had to make a guess about his return from the Hill. "My posting in the North East immediately followed a gruesome assignment during the Bangladesh war. As I told you earlier, I developed the problem of allergy to 'malarial antigens' during my posting in the Hills of the North-East region....."

I hardly remembered if he had earlier talked about the problem. He continued with his history: "My cough has started troubling me more ever after I assumed this office. I find it especially embarrassing when I need to meet people such as the Prime Minister or the President. I cannot afford to avoid those meetings." I did appreciate his problem but chose to ignore that statement. I interjected with a different line of questioning: "Sir, have you ever smoked?"

"I have never smoked. I am aware that smokers suffer from asthma, but not a person like me," he firmly asserted. He attributed his cough to the *malarial antigens* which he inhaled in his early days. His associates had given several examples of people suffering from cough after living in that region with high mosquito load. He was highly allergic to the issue of smoking. "The pollutants are deposited in my lungs", he always insisted. Any suggestion to the contrary was totally unacceptable.

"Doctor, I am convinced that the knowledge of the cause of allergy is essential for purposes of treatment", he posed to me. He insisted that he suffered from an allergy which doctors tried to misinterpret as asthma. He desired that allergy tests including for malarial antigens be done for him. "But Sir, malaria is not the likely cause for your present symptoms", I somehow managed to interject after listening to all his reasoning. I could perhaps take some liberties which others could not. Finally, a battery of several skin tests for common allergens was organized. The results were inconclusive. He did demonstrate allergic reactions to a few pollens and other proteins. It was not possible to specifically avoid the exposure to those agents. He was not even ready to consider a de-sensitization plan with allergen injections. The whole effort was a waste of time but it helped to stop his regular nagging. Slowly, he adjusted himself to the plan of medical treatment.

A contemporary Governor of another state had an almost opposite personality but for his similar attitude towards his own illness. He was a simple man but quite adamant in his thoughts. Older than our army Governor, he had held several positions of power in his long political career. He spoke little about his past experiences or encounters. It was a bit difficult to continue a prolonged discussion with him even in the presence of his personal physician.

Although he claimed to have recently stopped smoking, he had consumed "millions" of cigarettes in the past, in his own words. "Oh, ever since I recall I had a cigarette in my hand. I have been smoking since my childhood. I must have smoked millions of cigarettes. But now I have stopped smoking. Everybody has been after my cigarettes." He seemed to be rather proud of his smoking habit. He continued: "But that has nothing to do with my problem of cough. The problem of cough factually started after I stopped smoking."

"Sir, smoking is an important cause of cough", I tried to reason with him.

"But I have left smoking now – I have already told you so".

"It is rather a short period since you quit smoking. The effects are not going to go away so soon. It will be several more months, perhaps years before we expect some change. Moreover, a lot of changes in the lungs are irreversible to a large extent." I tended to put forward my scientific logic. I added further: "Meanwhile, we need to optimize drug treatment for the problem. We must protect the lungs from continued damage and try to minimize progression".

His chronic cough bothered his family more than himself. It was the occurrence of fever which brought him to the hospital. In spite of his age and multiple illnesses, he made a fairly good recovery. It was the post-hospitalization period which proved to be his nemesis. He became highly agitated and kept asking for a newer form of treatment for the 'phlegm in his lungs". His cough medications had multiplied. It took several months before he calmed down to his normal self.

Both the Governors were very sharp with their quick-witted replies. They could knock anybody off their feet in a minute. I found both of them as men of logic but for their own health. That has been a common trait of most of the VIP patients whom I have managed in the past few decades. Their opinions become difficult to challenge. I have always found it somewhat incongruous that some of the VIP patients tend to impose their own views during medical consultation with a doctor who is called in for that purpose. That is generally not so in case of a legal consultation from a lawyer.

I also found it difficult to examine senior politicians in private with satisfaction. They always loved to be accompanied by their assistants and security personnel.

Most of the times, the attendants would insist on staying and explain the patient's symptoms, sometimes more impulsively than the patient himself. I always felt embarrassed and severely handicapped by their presence. Slowly I learned the tactics from one of my surgeon friends. He explained that one had to politely tell the assistants that you needed to do an 'internal' examination. That was how the urologists and gynecologists would examine their VIPs. A routine medical examination was perhaps considered as innocuous, impersonal or benign.

The explanation with reference to internal examination succeeded many a time, but not always. It happened with one chief-minister who was always accompanied by two or three assistants, even in an examination room. While two of the assistants had moved out on my request, the third stayed back. I accepted his plea and let him stay. After all, I only needed to examine the chest, that too with my stethoscope. The assistant was considered necessary for removal of the minister's shirt.

One other difficulty of management was related to the prescription of inhalers. It was difficult to train an asthmatic chief minister or governor in inhalation techniques. Almost invariably, there was a kind of resentment the moment an inhaler was mentioned. One extremely soft spoken and otherwise cooperative chief minister had once joked that to learn to use an inhaler was more difficult for him than to handle the elected members of the legislative assembly aspiring for berths in the Ministry. The problem was compounded further by several different opinions on drug administration, offered unsolicited by others in the crowd.

The same chief minister was once admitted in the hospital for an acute problem. Many of us were worried at his poor compliance to treatment. We could manage his acute illness only with great difficulty. But the real test of patience came at the time of discharge. How to convince the honourable patient to continue with the maintenance treatment at home was a ticklish issue. I was pushed to act in an impolite manner even at the cost of my reputation. Taking his wife in confidence, I told him bluntly: "Sir, we hope that you would not like to visit us again and again in the hospital". He was equally humorous, replied mischievously: "It will be my pleasure to see you again". I spoke almost thoughtlessly: "But sir, we wish to see you continue at the helm of affairs". He gave a pleasant smile, promised to be more careful with his treatment. True to his words, he complied religiously. He was never admitted again.

A VIP himself could often end with substandard medical care from those doctors who played safe. This would lead to deviation from standard protocols especially when tough decisions were needed for invasive procedures or aggressive treatments. A tendency towards micro-dissection of treatment-decisions leading to either an over or under emphasis on side-effects and toxicities of treatments may also occur. Worst of all, there are too many well-wishers who assume the role of advising a 'better treatment'.

Gullibility in medicine is highly *infectious*. It catches you before you realize that you are exposed to falsehood. Yet you keep on believing what others suggest to you. Importantly, it is the belief which characterizes gullibility not the suggestion which can be either purposeful or just incidental. No better example can be found than the childhood puppet character Pinocchio who was repeatedly duped by the Fox and the Cat and others. In our example, both the Chief Ministers enjoyed discussion with the surrounding cronies. They would easily get swayed by suggestions of sycophants who were ever ready to please with different forms of stories or advice. Nonetheless, the *newer ideas* posed frequent problems for me and the medical teams. How can the people in highly responsible positions be so gullible?

The benefit of medical management multiply manifold if one understands the scientific basis of management. Incidentally, a disease does not differentiate between different groups of people. The basic principles of treatment are largely the same even though the affordability of different treatment options may significantly differ. Somehow, people in powerful positions consider an illness as a weakness. They either tend to hide the ailment or seek the unprofessional support of subordinates who are ready to oblige. That gullibility for sure is a greater weakness than the illness itself. Inadvertently, they tend to ignore professional advice. A short-term benefit may sometime accrue. It is only later in the course that the truth comes out. Both the Governors and the Chief Ministers at different points of time were advised by self-styled physicians to abandon regular therapy and try unproven remedies for cure. Consequently, both had suffered from exacerbations requiring hospitalization.

23.

MARITAL WOES

"Rakhi's marriage is due in about a week from now. Please provide some treatment to keep her free from regular medicine for at least a few months until after her marriage". Mrs. Goyal the mother pleaded. I felt a bit nervous at that request. Politely I told that we should not play with her treatment. She was not convinced. She further added: "You might give some strong medicine now. What will her in-laws think if they come to know of her asthma?"

"Did not you inform her husband and his family about her illness?" I asked with great skepticism. "How could we do so? The marriage would have never materialized if the fact was told to them", told Mrs. Goyal. I was not at all happy with that kind of deception. I was afraid that any such discontinuation of treatment would result in worsening. Rakhi was a young girl in her mid-twenties who used to regularly visit the clinic for the past several years. Her asthma was stable with regular treatment. But she used to worsen whenever she defaulted with her treatment. The mother was not at all happy with the need to continue with inhalers after the marriage. "Will they accept her in their family? Her husband will reject her"! Those were the fears frankly expressed by the deeply worried mother. I wished that she were equally frank with the people on the other side.

I could not accept her version of arguments. Marriage or no marriage, health was important. I faced a big dilemma in handling the situation - I could neither do wonders with Rakhi's treatment, nor let her suffer after her marriage. I did not wish at all to play a proactive role but offered to explain the condition to the future groom and his family. Rakhi was inclined but the mother was reluctant. She wanted some time to think it over. She promised to come back in a day or so. She did not return.

I had forgotten the incident but for the surprise visit of Rakhi after a few weeks of the earlier dialogue. Rakhi, in the full gear of a newly married bride was sitting in an adjoining room. Adorned with golden jewellery and arms full of *chooda* bangles, she was accompanied by her husband. She looked quite bright without any distress. She had now reported with a new hospital card. She was seen by one of the junior doctors who wanted to discuss her problems. She did not either notice me in that crowded surrounding or tried to feign her ignorance. It was obvious to me that that she was trying to pose herself as a new patient who developed the problem after her marriage. I had no obvious reason to interfere and carried on with my work as usual.

The issue seemed to die down soon until it haunted me again about a year ago when another young girl, Geeti was brought by her mother. She had been a bad patient of asthma with multiple complications. I had strongly advised the family against her marriage. But here she was in a similar dress as of Rakhi who I had seen earlier. Severely distressed, she was reported to be pregnant. I was told that Geeti had hard pressed her family for marriage. My second advice to get her pregnancy terminated also fell on deaf ears. She was quite compliant with drug-treatment but hardly prepared for any other advice. I had clearly expressed my fears related to the risks of continuing with her pregnancy to her mother. She as well made all kinds of pleas without caring for what I had to tell. Within the next few weeks, Geeti was admitted in the Intensive Care Unit of a local hospital with early onset of labour. She breathed her last after delivering a low birth-weight baby.

Both the incidents reflect the collective state of mind of our society on marriage. We can have better explanations on the phenomena from sociologists. Undoubtedly however, the presence of a chronic illness is a stigma for marriage. As a doctor, I have no clear solution in my mind. I know for sure that concealment of facts about the presence of disease proves to be highly detrimental. Hiding an illness is also cheating. Not infrequently, it results in legal suits and divorces. It is also an important cause of domestic violence, suicide and assault. Fortunately, asthma is a disease which on treatment is completely compatible with normal life.

Being privy to the confidential stories of people, it was sometimes amusing to note that both the partners had hidden the presence of known problems from each other. It was generally the severity of illness which determined the stability of marriage. Divulgence however is the most fair and truthful policy. It minimizes the follow up risks of fraud or other inter-personal conflicts.

Unlike Rakhi and Geeti, it was Sonika who proved to be a good example of woman emancipation. She was a bold girl who suffered from diabetes since her childhood.

She self-administered the insulin injections for control of her blood sugar levels every day. She would often visit the Chest Clinic for a minor cough which used to come and go. There was no apparent cause. Generally speaking, she was quite okay with her respiratory symptoms. It puzzled me as to why she would come so frequently and waste her time in waiting. One day, I came to know that rather than wasting, it was time well spent. The true story was revealed by her mother who came with a box of sweets in the Clinic. Sonika was engaged to Amar who used to bring his mother to the Clinic.

Sonika after entering the third decade of her life was looking for a partner with whom she could share her life. Her parents were rather skeptical but they agreed not to raise an objection in case she could find a willing boy. Who would accept a newly married bride in regular need for the life-saving drug? Success came rather unexpectedly, at a highly unlikely place in the waiting hall of the hospital. Amar and Sonika became friends while waiting for their turns.

Sonika's mother was elated as she narrated the story of their courtship. "Will you marry me?" Amar had proposed to Sonika one day. Sonika was not ready for the question. She had clearly replied: "I have got diabetes which is there to stay for my life." You see, she did not hide a single fact. Amar was a very intelligent boy. He knew everything. He had himself told: "I myself had suffered from tuberculosis in the past. I got cured with treatment. The scars in my lungs do trouble me occasionally. Worse still, I cannot get rid of that stigma".

Sonika had happily consented. They soon got married at a simple ceremony. That day, I realized that misery could be unravelled by the purest feelings of the mind. Hospitals could therefore equally well serve as meeting points for lovers in distress.

The duo of Sonika and Amar remained happy for as long as I know. They did occasionally visit the hospital for disease related problems. Together they could efficiently manage their difficulties. Most importantly, they well understood their individual needs. Wisely so, they adopted an infant girl from a local orphanage. It was rather sad that a folly on the part of Geeti and her mother had ended in disastrous consequences. Rakhi was lucky in spite of the wrong path which she took.

24.

THE STIGMA OF INDERJEET

Inderjeet's joy knew no bounds when she passed her Civil Services competition examination with an excellent grade and qualified for selection as an officer in the Indian Police Service. She could now hope to fulfil her long cherished ambition to serve as an officer in the Indian Police. There was only one more step to achieve that goal i.e. the mandatory medical fitness clearance by the Medical Board.

As luck would have it, she started with general malaise along with pain in the lower back a few days before she was due for the medical fitness test. Apprehending medical problems, her father, a former soldier himself, consulted an *orthopedic* surgeon. Detailed investigations including the x-rays and magnetic resonance imaging done for the spine revealed the problem. There was a small collection of some amount of fluid along the spine. Fortunately, there was no apparent destruction of vertebrae.

The diagnosis caused a huge disappointment for the whole family, especially for the girl and her father. They almost lapsed into a state of severe depression. She was referred to me for commencement of treatment. She was also advised to avoid exertion to prevent an unintended injury to the spine. Inderjeet got her medical examination postponed on grounds of temporary sickness. The family was shell-shocked into silence. But the period which followed proved to be rather nasty.

The girl was isolated in a small room in the house. No one was allowed to visit except her mother and an old maid who was known to be highly loyal. One of them would serve her food and provide essential items for her day to day needs. They did not talk to anyone else about her illness. On the other hand, there was a concerted effort to spread word in the neighbour-hood that the girl has been sent for training to some far-off center.

Diagnosis of tuberculosis was a stigma in the past. It aroused fear of contagion in the community. But the response of Inderjeet's family was highly anomalous for this decade. Inderjeet was one of the several millions of ordinary citizens of India who suffered from tuberculosis of one or the other organ. Factually, she was one of the more fortunate individuals who could be saved unlike the renowned celebrities of the past including kings and queens.

Totally deprived of the company of friends, Inderjeet immersed herself in her lap-top. The real facts dawned upon her as soon as she started surfing on the internet. It was clear to her that her compulsory isolation to one room was mostly erroneous. She started confronting her parents with information gathered from her computer. She had previously read the famous book '*The Magic Mountain*' by Thomas Mann. She did not wish to suffer the fate of *Hans Castorp* the protagonist of The Magic Mountain. *Hans Castorp* had to suffer in a sanatorium for seven years after being diagnosed with tuberculosis. Inderjeet decided to escape the 'prison' on her own.

But better sense prevailed upon the father who agreed to end the period after 10-12 days of isolation. The duo came back to the Institute for further advice. It was almost for the first time that they frankly talked of tuberculosis. Until that time, they had scrupulously avoided a direct reference to the terminology even though the treatment was actually in place from the earlier visit. Both Inderjeet and her father had a large number of doubts in their minds. It was not easy for them to accept that a young lady could develop the "obnoxious disease", in spite of a healthy life-style.

"Doctor Sahib, are you sure of the diagnosis? Tuberculosis as I know is a *disease of the slums*. God has given us plenty to live a happy life. *My daughter* eats a hearty meal every day?" The father seemed to be rather skeptical. He continued: "She does not have any bad habit of smoking or drinking, does her regular exercises. She has full blessings of *Waheguru*." The father's questions were hard to answer.

"Please be assured. There is hardly a doubt about the illness. Victims of tuberculosis include people from all walks of life. A number of kings, princes, scientists, authors and actors had suffered from tuberculosis in the 19th and early 20th century. Even today, we have eminent people from all walks of life as our patients." I tried to explain to his satisfaction.

"But how has she sinned? She bows before the Guru every day. She says her prayers in the early morning." The father continued to harp upon the theme of sinning. That made me a little edgy. I gave him a long lecture. To cut it short, I firmly retorted: "A disease is not a sin. Do not minimize the strengths of your daughter. You should be proud of your daughter as one of the few brave officers in the Indian Police."

He seemed to mellow down and did not speak any further. After a long pause, he put forward a more mundane question: "Is it not true that patients with TB have cough, sputum and fever? Inderjeet has none of those features. Moreover, she never had bleeding from her lungs. But for some pain, she seems to be healthy."

"True. But Inderjeet does not have tuberculosis of the lungs. You need not worry about those issues. Absence of one or the other symptom does not imply the absence of disease". I tried to be brief in replying. I am not sure if he understood the explanation, but he did not make any further query. On the other hand, Inderjeet armed with information from the internet, did not have many doubts. Most importantly, she had learnt that the disease could be permanently cured.

It is not commonly appreciated by both the medical and the lay public alike that tuberculosis of spine is perhaps the most ancient form of tuberculosis. The portraits of hunchbacks pictured by the Egyptian artists on the walls of over 5000 year old tombs are considered to suggest tubercular vertebral destruction. Remnants of skeletal tuberculosis have been found in the Neolithic Mediterranean and Ancient Egyptian mummies. It is also said that the queen Nefertiti and her husband king Akhenaten of ancient Egypt died of tuberculosis. The presence of skeletal tuberculosis was substantiated further by the examination of a well preserved Egyptian "mummy" of 3400 B.C. in whom the vertebral destruction and an associated abscess could be clearly ascertained. Inderjeet's case seemed to be almost similar but for the absence of vertebral destruction.

Since antiquity, tuberculosis is known to involve humans and animals alike. Direct or indirect reference to tuberculosis can be found in ancient literature of most of the old civilizations. Many ancient texts such as *'The code of Hammurabi' of Babylon,* the medical papyri of Egypt, the Laws of Manu and the Rig-Veda of Indo-Aryan period – all of the pre-biblical era - clearly mention about the disease in different descriptions. Lung tuberculosis can be found only in the later writings of the Chinese, Babylonian and Indo Aryan literature of 2600-1500 BC era, about 1-2 millennia later than the skeletal tuberculosis. Body consumption and contagious nature are the two important characteristics which have been pointed out.

Although the disease was better understood at the end of the 19th century when Robert Koch discovered the responsible micro-organism i.e. the tubercle bacillus, the fear as well as the stigma persisted. Such was the degree of fear that when the famous English poet John Keats discovered blood in his sputum in his early twenties, he wrote: "That blood is my death warrant, I must die". It was only in the latter half of the 20th century that it became possible to cure tuberculosis after the discovery of anti-tubercular drugs.

A great deal of discussion on the illness helped to erase the stigma from their minds. The girl was confident that she would soon recover. The parents were repentant for their misgivings which had added on to the misery. The father later confided in me that he felt let down by the girl's illness. "She would have been rejected for recruitment in the Police", he clearly verbalized. "It was impossible for me to accept that my daughter – a soldier's offspring, had been declared a patient of tuberculosis." He further added: "You do not know *doctor sahib*. Army used to send a soldier back home the moment the diagnosis of tuberculosis was suspected. The mere mention of tuberculosis could make us jobless. We would hide our symptoms at all costs. We would forcibly keep cough suppressed in front of officers. Moreover, I could not tolerate her colleagues running away from her."

Trying to encourage him further, I consoled: "Inderjeet did not have cough. Her disease was factually not infectious for others." He replied with confidence; "I now know the truth. I am all prepared to face the future consequences."

Inderjeet continued to come for follow up visits on regular basis. She had completely recovered from her illness, gained adequate weight and muscle strength. She had also gone through intensive physical training after a few months of treatment. She could again run and participate in other strenuous exercises. It was after about a year later when she gave the good news of her appointment after the Medical Board had declared her physically fit. "I am completely cured of tuberculosis. I do not carry the stigma any more". She almost shouted with great joy! I thought that this was a matter of ignorance and false pride.

25.

UNIVERSITY DONS

Panjab University, located opposite to the Medical Institute across a central road, the *Madhya Marg*, is one of finest in the country. Established originally in 1882 at Lahore in the undivided Punjab, it shifted to various locations in Punjab after the partition of India in 1947. Finally, it got relocated to its present address in Chandigarh in 1956. The University prides itself for its red stone campus designed by Pierre Jeanneret, a celebrated Swiss architect who collaborated with his cousin, Charles Edouard Jeanneret (Le Corbusier) in giving the city a distinctly modern look which is unlike most other cities of India. Some of the structures such as the monumental *Gandhi Bhawan* and the rotund Students' Centre vie to be listed as heritage sites. There is an excellent Fine Arts museum and a botanical garden besides the usual teaching blocks, auditoria, swimming pool and play grounds. Its wide roads are lined by lush green trees on both sides.

The Students' Centre which housed a popular restaurant had always attracted us from the Medical Institute in the early decades when the food joints were rather few in the city. During my formative years, I had frequently enjoyed a walk in the campus of the University in the late evening after finishing my work in the hospital wards. That was almost always followed by a South Indian *dosa* dinner. This relationship with the University, established during the residency period, continued to grow later. I subsequently developed friendship with several of the teachers of different departments of the University.

Panjab University had some excellent departments in which various research scholars were engaged in work on different subjects including in biomedical specialties. It provided an ideal environ for the learning of basic sciences. I also participated in a few joint research projects in collaboration with the university faculty. More importantly however, I remained in touch with many a university teacher for different kinds of medical consultation. Faculty as well students would visit the Institute in times of sickness. They were always my privileged patients whenever they needed any help.

As a teacher myself, I share many qualities or characteristics with university teachers. I have learnt a great deal interacting with them on different occasions. University teachers had always commanded respect in the city. In all fairness, I must say that we envied them greatly. While we at the PGI remained unusually preoccupied with work, the University Faculty enjoyed a lot of free time. At least that was what most of us believed!

Teachers and doctors have different theories for their illnesses. They formulate their own hypotheses and concepts. It always required immense patience and time to argue with a University don, more so to get your point accepted. Frequently, it made a treatment plan difficult, sometimes even disappointing.

Professor Ahuja was a senior faculty member of a science department. He, along with his wife, met me in my office in the late afternoon. Prof. Ahuja had a brief history of about 24 hours of dry cough and a vague feeling of malaise. There was associated chest pain which was followed by a single bout of blood stained sputum. In view of his age and background history I suspected the occurrence of a blood clot in his lung circulation but I needed a few investigations to pinpoint the diagnosis. His symptomatology required immediate attention for which he was required to stay in the hospital.

To avoid a scare, I proposed the possibility of a blood clot in rather milder terms: "Either a small blood clot or an infection due to pneumonia may have caused your problem. There is nothing to worry. We should..." Before I could complete my statement, he interjected, "Oh no doctor. I am not worried at all. I had my Honours' class in the morning. Just give me some medicine to let me sleep well".

"Some urgent tests are quite in order. It could well be a simple infection", I tried to impress upon them the need to stay.

"But why should I develop pneumonia? He asked. "I have been quite healthy. I do not smoke or drink"

He seemed to me like Bill Maher, an American advocate who would blame everything else but germs as causes of infection. He came to be famously or infamously known as the 'germ-theory denier'. Irritated at the constant denial of logic by Professor Ahuja, I tried to end the discussion: "But you do have a problem, whatever the reason. Let us be sure of the diagnosis first. Rest of the things can wait."

Unmindful of my restlessness, he continued to argue about the futility of tests. "Why can't I be treated at home? I have heard of so many hospital-acquired infections."

I wished I were blunt in my answers. Somehow, I could not offend my friend Dr. Sharma who had called me earlier to personally see to Professor Ahuja. I tried to be reasonable lest he decide to go back home. Most importantly, I did not wish the bleeding to happen again, not outside the hospital in any case. A second episode would have been frightening besides being unmanageable at home.

"We shall try to shorten your hospitalization to the minimum period. It could well be tuberculosis or even an unusual presentation of a blood clot in one of the vessels of the lung". I tried to impress upon the need of admission and investigations.

"How can bleeding happen if the vessel is blocked due to clots? It is not going to happen now. Please let me sleep at home. I am quite exhausted."

I was exhausted myself. Before I could call it quits, his wife intervened. "Doctor Sahib, you please don't listen to him. It is quite his habit to keep debating. No risk-taking. We are ready for admission." She seemed to know better than Professor Ahuja. "How shall we handle the problem at night in case of a recurrence?" She was obviously worried of an impending emergency. "For God's sake, the infection should not be serious."

The professor was not ready to lose ground, "But why infection? I was not exposed to anybody with a similar infection". The nagging discussion between husband and wife continued for some time with me as a mute spectator. Finally, the don agreed to stay in the hospital. The couple went home to get the essentials for hospitalization.

I left instructions with the medical resident regarding his admission late in the evening. However, he did not report until early morning next day. My friend Dr. Sharma who had referred him earlier called me again to inform that Professor Ahuja needed critical care. He had a sudden episode of severe breathlessness. He was almost gasping for breath. The doctor at the University Health Centre had given some emergency injections to settle him down. I was also told that Professor Ahuja after visiting me had consulted at least two more doctors including a famous Homeopathic physician in the city. Various types of drugs were administered. He had hoped to recover but worsened overnight.

Fortunately, he soon settled down after admission. As suspected, he was detected to have developed clotting of blood in his lungs. He was discharged after appropriate treatment. He did not raise any doubt during hospitalization. But he never accepted the fact that he was wrong. While leaving the hospital, he thanked me for all the help. His final departing comments reflected a sense of defensiveness. He remarked, "Actually, I did not really need an admission. My bleeding had settled. Even breathing had been easier following treatment at the University Centre. My wife decided to bring me to the hospital. You know the psychology of women. They get unduly worried at small incidents."

His remarks left me speechless. How could I tell him that his wife had brought him back from the hands of *yamaraj* – the god of death? Married Hindu women in

Northern India passionately celebrate *Karva Chauth* by reminding themselves of the story of a faithful wife. In all different versions, the central theme is related to a wife's assiduous fast and stern refusal to allow *Yama* to take away the body of the husband. *Yama* has to finally yield and give back life to the husband. In the present case, a large clot could have been fatal for Professor Ahuja. All my advice seemed to have vanished in thin air. I chose to ignore his observations by reconciling with what Stephen Hunt had believed: "Even a broken clock is right twice a day."

Of course, most of the dons were unlike Professor Ahuja. Generally speaking, they were excessively concerned with illnesses as well as treatments. Heart disease was their most common obsession with cancer the next most feared illness. Even ordinary complaints got unduly exaggerated, sometimes entirely manufactured. Vikram, a lecturer in Mathematics used to regularly visit the Institute for his "potential heart attack". Each time he would try to impress with an observation that the "chest congestion this time is different than the earlier one". "Dr. Jindal, I am afraid that I may have really suffered a heart attack" he would repeat in different words every few months.

Vikram had a legendary collection of electrocardiograms, each done during such an episode of chest discomfort. But for the fact that they were normal, the number of ECGs which he invariably brought with him could have been used as teaching exercises for the medical students. Each time, he would try to insist upon evaluation of previous ECGs for purpose of comparison. I had to find different excuses to escape from that examination. Surprisingly, each normal ECG would assure him in continuing with his habit of smoking. "Thank God, it is normal. I had feared to find an abnormality in my ECG this time. It seems I am safe for the present." My repeated advice to get rid of that root cause of heart attacks failed repeatedly. Each time he would agree with my mundane advice with his standard reply: "I do promise to quit next time". I had always wondered as to when the 'next time' would come.

I believe that highly educated people tend to develop an aggravated form of self- confidence. Rather than searching for explanations for problems they start fitting problems into their explanations. They tend to 'rule in' or 'rule out' a disease purely on the basis of their knowledge gathered from multiple sources which could be partly factual and partly fictional. An advice contrary to one's own view-point is dismissed as casual and incorrect. Electronic media, particularly the internet is easy to refer to in case of a doubt. One can always find some material in support of a particular view point. There is no comprehensive analysis of evidence. Subsequently, decisions are based on hearsay and on anecdotal examples rather than systematic studies. This type of decision-making is extremely faulty and fraught with risks of serious consequences.

A doctor behaves in a similar fashion when an illness relates to him or her. A retired Head of a department of the Institute had considered a small lesion on her chest x-ray as inconsequential. Not taking any notice of medical advice given to her, she quietly sat at home. She chose to get further investigations almost a year later. The small nodule which was detected in the past had advanced into an inoperable lung cancer. Similarly, a resident doctor in the department of Pathology had developed typical symptoms of fever, weakness and weight loss. He got a chest x-ray done but failed to pursue it further. He attributed all those symptoms to prolonged duty hours and erratic food intake. He never bothered to seek an alternate explanation till about a few weeks later. He consulted me when he noticed blood in the sputum. The previous chest x-ray itself was found to have gross abnormalities. He had never bothered to show the film to either a radiologist or a physician. The diagnosis of tuberculosis was easy to make but the treatment was fairly delayed. He passed through a difficult time but did recover after the initial hiccups.

It is not important to cite the numerous similar examples physicians face in day to day clinical practice. It is only fair to conclude that there is no substitute to professional expertise. The level of education alone is not necessarily a determinant of a correct medical decision. Evidence always outweighs manufactured arguments – howsoever strong an argument may look like. Secondly, a self-determined option of treatment is the right of an individual but not generally correct. One always tends to opt for an easier option. On the other hand, a professional medical advice may be difficult to swallow but is more likely to be correct.

26.

SWAMI ANAND

Swami Anand was sick with multiple health problems. He was admitted in the Private Wards of the Institute for his uncontrolled diabetes and a heart ailment. He had developed constant cough following an episode of fever which lasted for about 2-3 weeks. He was quite distressed because of his symptoms although he tried to present a cheerful look. "I am doing very well after the treatment given to me. My friends are unnecessarily disturbed," he tried to mask the discomfort through which he was going. The friends he referred to were his followers or other well-wishers who had brought him to the hospital. I had already received a few calls from several senior people in the city including a few from the Institute inquiring into his health. I was not quite sure about the background of *Swamiji*. The very first meeting with him proved to be quite satisfying and removed a lot of bias from my mind. I had always felt a bit uncomfortable if multiple people posed questions about the health of an individual with whom they were not directly concerned. The concern appeared artificial in most cases.

The eighty two year old *Swamiji* had a long tale of his journey through life to tell to me. The medical problems were only occasionally interposed in our conversation. The story started with his birth in Punjab in a town not distant from my own home place. More interestingly, he had taught in a College in Patiala for several years – a city where I had studied for my graduation in medicine. He did not marry but left his home to join an *Ashram* where he stayed as a sadhu. Thereafter he wandered all around the globe in different places including in several Ram Krishna Ashrams. He had travelled in over a hundred different countries including America where he used to spend a lot of time at the *Ashram* run by an international Foundation in Chicago. Swamiji had also spent some time with Mother Teressa in Kolkata whom he described as extremely kind and merciful.

I later learnt that Mr. Jaiswal, one of his followers, who often accompanied Swamiji during visits, and ran a Foundation in the United States, originally belonged to the same region as the *swamiji*. That must had been at least one of the reasons behind a close association. He had done his early schooling from my own childhood-city, Dhuri. I also came to know that he was my contemporary, though he had studied at a different school.

It was obvious to me that Swami Anand possessed a vast experience of different cultures across the world. He understood human relationships as they existed in different societies more intricately than I did. However, I had the advantage when it came to the state of an illness. It was not surprising to see how an ailment could make one weak and dependent. Even a learned saint enlightened in the deeper secrets of the philosophy of life felt disappointed when a serious illness struck. The fear of death is always a haunting experience for a sick person, be it the rich or the poor, the ordinary or the elite. The degree of this fear is however variable. It does not depend upon the level of formal education. The learned and the saintly people may find sickness as more acceptable and reasonable than common people. Even that is not always so. The elite may find a disease as even more unwelcome.

Swami Anand was remarkably successful in hiding his fears from those around him. He had the knack of shifting the focus of discussion from his illness to the virtues of wellbeing. Rather than exaggerating, he would try to minimize his symptoms to make everyone else comfortable. Besides his spirituality, what impressed me most was his confidence in the modern approach to disease-management. Medicine has somehow become an anathema for many a celebrated saint. Unlike others, Swami Anand considered medicine as an important medium to win back health. He advocated early medicinal treatment rather than wasting time and supported his contention with examples from different scriptures in addition to the logic of science: "In *Ramayana, Bhagwan Rama* himself had wanted the *sanjeevni booti* to be brought at the earliest for treatment of *Lakshmana who fell unconscious when struck with an arrow in his battle with Meghnath, the son of the demon king, Ravana."* A disease is an unnatural state which cannot be effectively handled without the administration of medicine".

That somehow has not been a common trait. I have had the chance to face a good many saints or sadhus of different faiths. Though I do not intend to find faults in their sects or beliefs, it was rather intriguing to find their aversion, sometimes amounting to antagonism, to modern medicine - the so called 'artificial approach for disease-management'.

This was despite the fact that almost everyone had significantly benefited from modern medicine, especially during acute phases of their illnesses or in emergencies. More than one had undergone some kind of surgical procedure, for example the heart bye-pass surgery, appendicectomy, angioplasty or the like.

Swami Anand always considered it a kind of hypocrisy to preach something which he did not practice. He had nothing to say in case one did not believe in modern medical intervention. But it had been his firm conviction that one must be able to apply the same principles of management to one's own problems as one tells others to adopt. One must live up to the standards one advocates and preaches others to live up to.

Equally so, we the medical practitioners believe that medicine is a do-all remedy for an illness. Not always so. Spirituality and faith add to the options of management. They also multiply the benefits of medical treatment. Spirituality has great bearing in medical practice as much as in one's life. To understand the role of spirituality, Dr. N.N. Wig, a senior Professor of Psychiatry at the Institute, used to quote from the Chinese book of Wisdom by Tao Te Ching –

> We join spokes together in a wheel,
> but it is the central hole
> that makes the wagon move.
> We shape clay into a pot,
> but it is the emptiness inside
> that holds whatever we want.
> We hammer wood for house,

but it is the inner space
that makes it livable.
We work with being,
but non-being is what we use.

Swami Anand for that matter was a man of a different class. He advocated a combined approach of spirituality with physical treatments. Spirituality for him involved belief in whatever you adopt. He himself presented a perfect example of a practicing sadhu who did not differentiate between his beliefs for others as for himself. He was not a self-styled god-man with a large following. I however considered him an ideal example of a spiritual practitioner, way beyond a larger number of eminent god-men. His relaxed and simplistic attitude to life reinforced the importance of spirituality in our day to day medical practice. I always felt that his approach had a significantly positive appeal for an ill individual. It was also proof of how a spiritually strong individual could overcome the pains of an illness.

Following an intensive course of therapy, Swami Anand was soon out of the bed to go back to his Mission to continue with his work for the people. He could never rest without work. I greatly admired the three vows he was administered by his guru: Spirituality is a personal value, never enforce those values upon others in your public discourses; do not seek favours from powerful people as a price of your goodness, and do not let others fall to your feet. The Swami scrupulously kept the promises he had made and maintained his dignity in front of those who cared to come to him. He never let his followers touch his feet. He was one Swami who had followed the righteous path of service.

27.

THE DEVILISH TEST

High 'erythrocyte sedimentation rate' had not been bothersome only for Aman and Sarup Kaur (mentioned earlier) who used to repeatedly visited the clinic, but for several other patients, in at least some of whom the test could be blamed for more serious problems. There were numerous other examples of 'abnormal tests' of little clinical significance causing sleepless nights for anxious patients. Truly speaking, the tests are quite innocent, and only serve the best interests of the patients. We can blame the computer which reads the test, or the human mind which interprets results according to its own convenience. Without going into the scientific merits of one such investigation, I would like to cite the case of Prakash whose marriage was seriously threatened due to a positive skin test for tuberculosis. Families of both the bride and the bridegroom had remained at loggerheads for no good reason.

Prakash, who enjoyed all the privileges of an upper-middle class family of Chandigarh, was a postgraduate student at a local college, who dreamt to make it big in his life. He had plans to go for a higher education degree in business administration and later to start his personal capital venture in due course of time. He got engaged to his classmate Kalpana after a brief courtship. Kalpana was a pampered girl, who to a great extent had a similar background. Whatever she wanted was made available to her by her parents. She had hardly ever faced failure or disappointment. It seemed that they both were made for each other. Even though they had developed a spontaneous friendship, the engagement was more of an arranged liaison with the mutual understanding of the two families. They matched very well when examined by the *pandits* of the two families. This was also confirmed with the help of computer-generated *Kundlies*. Everyone involved was happy and excited. Both Kalpana and Prakash were keenly looking for the D-day to arrive soon.

A few weeks before the marriage, Prakash developed an episode of loose motions along with fever. There was a significant loss of appetite during that period. The problems persisted for a few days. He also complained of weakness which compelled him to take rest at home. He had never faced any such illness in the past. Concerned with the illness, the family took him to a doctor, who in addition to administering some medicine, got a few tests done. It was rather incidental that the doctor also ordered for the popular *Mantoux (Tuberculin) skin test*. The test is commonly done as one of several different investigations for diagnosis of the cause of prolonged fever and many other problems. In India, the test is positive in almost half of the normal adult population. Therefore, routinely we do not attach much importance to a positive test. Prakash soon recovered from his gastrointestinal upset. But all hell broke loose when

Mantoux test was reported as positive after 72 hours of the initial skin injection.

The news of the illness including the positive test travelled from Prakash himself to Kalpana and soon thereafter to her parents who got immensely agitated. The blame game started with one party accusing the other. A lot of bad blood passed between the two families. Kalpana's parents blamed Prakash that he hid the information about the serious disease to marry her for greed. Prakash's parents were scornful at the obnoxious behaviour of *that reprehensible family.* "It was that obstinate girl who hankered after my son. He is one in a million. We should have never agreed in the first place" said the angry mother to her friends. The situation fast turned into a typical Bollywood drama. Fortunately, there was no direct confrontation between members of the two families.

Fully recovered from his fever, Prakash was soon up and about. It was after about a week that his mother gave him the *good news of getting rid of that pesky family.* "So what if they own a bigger bungalow or a few more cars. We are in no way less than them" she tried to console her son who was stunned. He had no clue to the hostility which seemed to have developed within the short period of his illness. He could neither reconcile with the information which he gathered from his mother nor confront Kalpana with whom he was deeply attached. A break looked imminent since things had gone a little too far. However, he was not at all ready to loose in that fashion and decided to take things in his own hands.

When he contacted Kalpana, she was furious to know of the developments behind her back. Distressed at the unreasonable behaviour, she was ready to go ahead with the earlier plan of marriage against the wishes of her parents. Still both of them decided to tell their parents to amicably resolve the issue. The parents had little choice but the fear of tuberculosis continued to haunt like a hanging sword. Alternative solutions were suggested to postpone the marriage or quietly let both go abroad. Nothing seemed to be mutually acceptable. Someone finally came up with the idea of a consultation with a medical specialist at the Postgraduate Institute to assess the real situation. Both the aggrieved parties finally agreed with the proposed solution.

I was contacted by an eminent citizen interested in both the families. He told me that 'a boy' has been diagnosed to suffer from tuberculosis but wanted me to assure the girl's family about the boy's health. How could I take sides in case of a marital (or premarital) dispute? Initially I flatly refused to intervene. Later on, after repeated entreaties, I reluctantly agreed to look into the case to provide the real picture to my friend who had contacted me on behalf of the two parties. I had no good knowledge of the situation till that time. Being a doctor, I did not want to assume the role of a judge. I clearly told them that an honest opinion could well be bitter.

The problem was simpler than what I had expected and became clear to me when I studied the case history and looked into details. I could make my decision rather quickly with a good amount of confidence. He was one of the several hundred million people of this country who develop a positive skin reaction to tuberculin following their exposure to tuberculosis germs or to the BCG vaccination routinely administered to children in India. In countries with a high prevalence of tuberculosis, a positive *Mantoux test* could not be considered as an evidence of active tuberculosis. In spite of the known pitfalls of the test, misinterpretation continues amongst the lay public and doctors alike. Prakash also became a victim of ignorance, thus subject to the stigma of tuberculosis.

The clue provided by me was enough for my friend to build his case of arbitration. He made an impeccable plea with convincing arguments. He must have used several ingenious examples of his own to convince the two families who soon relented from their original stand. I met the girl and her parents separately to discuss the issue. They had several queries to which I patiently responded. I tried my best to clarify the doubts raised by them including those of the risks to Kalpana, the other members in the family and to the future progeny. The mother also wanted to know if there was a greater possibility of contracting tuberculosis in the years to come. It was rather tough to firmly commit on what could happen in the future. One had to know a bit of astrology to reply to some of the questions! I gave a standard answer to the queries about future risks: "Who can definitely predict that an accident will not happen while driving on a road? Some degree of risk cannot be totally avoided. The future prevention lies in our own hands".

'A drowning man will even clutch at a straw.' Kalpana took the lead thereafter and made her parents comfortable with her own arguments. The whole episode ended with a happy note; the acute phase of the illness as well as of acrimonies was over. The marriage was celebrated with great fervour. I earned a dinner invitation to the marriage, which I could not attend. A few years later, my arbitrator-friend informed me one day that Kalpana and Prakash were

happily married and had a lovely daughter who enjoyed comforts similar to what her mother got in her childhood. Perhaps I also enjoyed my part as a counsellor and felt that possibly I could earn my living as a marriage counsellor or an arbitrator. One can never be sure about a future role!

Meanwhile, the tuberculin test initially developed by the French physician Charles Mantoux, remains as popular as it was over a century ago. Even though its significance in clinical medicine continues to be riddled with controversies, its importance seems to have further grown in the current era following a rush for immigration to the West. A number of Western countries are not inclined to issue visas to people with positive tuberculin tests. That ensures that the test will continue to occupy an eminent place in the battery of medical investigations.

28.

YASIN MOHAMMAD

I recognized Yasin Mohammad at the Rose Festival at Chandigarh, during his performance with a dancing bear. The famous festival of roses is regularly held in the city in the Rose Garden, during the months of February or March to celebrate the bloom of roses every year. The *Zakir Hussain Rose Garden* located in the heart of the city, is perhaps the largest in Asia with around 1600 different varieties of roses. The annual activity has now been rechristened as the Festival of Gardens to expand the locale to multiple gardens. Besides the multiple varieties of roses, there has always been a splendid display of other flowers of the season. It is always a feast to walk through the rows of plants and appreciate the beauty of the huge, 'double' chrysanthemums, butterfly like pansies and colourful ranunculus. One can also find large columns of multi-coloured marigolds and petunias as well as enjoy the flower arrangements set by different competitors. The festival invariably draws huge crowds from the region.

On that day, there were special attractions for people of all ages which included the competition games, animal-rides and jugglery shows. Camel rides, rope-walking, monkey-tricks and bear-dance were going on and were proving to be particularly popular amongst children. I along with my family was having a nice Sunday, enjoying the pan Indian cuisine available at the festival. It was rather incidental that I saw Yasin Mohammad in one of the enclosure. He was exhibiting a bear who was dancing on his commands. Nearby, his 5-6 year old son was skilfully performing balancing acts in the air on a rope.

I stayed till the end of the dance to meet Yasin. He was one of my patients who had recently visited the clinic for worsening of his asthma. I wished to congratulate him on his performance. He was pleased with my words of praise but felt embarrassed at being noticed. On his own, he started murmuring different excuses– "I am a poor man sir! I have no other source of income. This bear provides me work and food to live!" I felt somewhat guilty. Why did he need to give an explanation? Perhaps he did not disclose his true occupation in the hospital. May be he felt that his profession was not up to the mark. I had no intention to ridicule him or his profession. I was well aware that a few of my patients were engaged in professions similar to that of Yasin in one or the other way. I assured him of my appreciation for his hard work. His son was well trained as an acrobat although I felt sorry that he did not go to school. He was too young to spend his time on the road.

With an expression of gratefulness for entertaining us I wanted to pay my dues like other spectators. He flatly refused to accept money in spite of the fact that he was working hard for each rupee. He let all of us have a hand-shake with the bear which though a bit scary was quite exciting. But the bear's hand was limp and slimy to feel.

He again visited the hospital a few days later after the festival was over. He was shown to me by the medical resident who had taken his history. The resident was trying to dig into the presence of an aggravating factor for the worsening in his asthma. When the resident had inquired about the possibility of a regular contact with pets or other animals, Yasin had skilfully hid the facts, but I knew the truth. It was quite possible that his close companion was responsible for his asthma. However, the pet was the only source of his income. I felt awfully sorry for Yasin. I could not gather the courage to discuss the issue with him. I could neither advise him to leave his profession nor to live with his 'pet'. I left it to the resident doctor to spend some time to dwell on it further.

Yasin had intelligently judged the dilemma we were facing in his case. "I love my bear like my own son" he repeatedly assured. He tried to comfort us by promising that he would get rid of his bear. That I knew was a false promise. He could not have easily changed his job. He knew nothing else than the bear dance. The profession ran in his tribal blood. He did feel happy following the treatment prescribed to him. That was the most one could do in those circumstances.

Years later, the taming of wild animals including bears, was made unlawful to prevent the cruel practices involved in their training. The bear cubs were known to be roped through the nose, separated from their mothers and treated brutally in order to be tamed. Bear baiting, which involved setting dogs on a tied bear was rumoured to occur occasionally. The practice was known to exist in neighbouring Pakistan but the charge was never substantiated in India. There had been persistent pressure by animal lovers. This was an obvious anathema in a modern civil society. Ms Menaka Gandhi, the celebrated animal rights activist, in her capacity as India's Animal Welfare Minister imposed a ban on use of bears and big cats in public performances. The ban not only affected the bear-shows but also animal performances in circuses. I do not know what subsequently happened to Yasin Mohammad. He disappeared into oblivion long before the law came into enforcement.

Petty favours rendered by ordinary, unrecognizable patients like Yasin have been enjoyable experiences for me. Those wonderful moments of pleasure have been as rewarding as an e-mail confirming the acceptance of a research paper for publication in an important professional Journal. I gleefully remember an old incidence which happened during one of my summer-holiday trips in Himachal Pradesh. My family and I were travelling on a hot after-noon. We were deadly tired of our journey along the circular hilly road and wanted to take some rest at a road-side tea-shop. It seemed there was none for miles to come.

It felt like the discovery of a hidden treasure when we spotted a small lonely 'dhaba' after a long drive some 300 kilometers away from Chandigarh. There were very few customers at that hour of the day. We immediately decided to stop for a hot cup of tea, whatever the facilities. There were a few old cots spread at the front which were made available to us to lie in case we wanted to relax. The long-route truck-drivers often preferred the cots. Though we opted for chairs, our preferred option proved to be tricky. Most of the wooden chairs had seats which were worn out.

The metallic chairs of tin made crackling sounds but were safer to sit on.

There was a hustle and bustle the moment we landed at the place. While one young lad came with a wet duster to clean the table, the other brought glasses along with a jug of water. Without bothering for hygiene, we gulped down the contents. We all were extremely thirsty. Soon thereafter, the tea-shop owner himself came for the order. Before I could utter a word, he burst out with pleasure. He was excited when he saw me. He was one of my old 'customers' who was highly satisfied with the services he had received at the medical institute. He was cured from an illness which 'none else' could handle before he landed with us.

He started showering praise on the medical services he had received during his admission. "You had given me a second life. You are next to God for me. It is my great fortune that you have visited this small man's place". I felt uncomfortable listening to him but he seemed to be quite serious in his expressions. He left no stone unturned to serve us well, poured us tea which was more sweet than his words. There was no scope left for any complaint. I wanted an additional cup of tea without sugar. He was surprised at the request but conceded after my insistence. Our tiredness soon disappeared with the hospitality he had shown. My ego got boosted many folds. I could not recall the past details of his illness. Perhaps he had suffered from a lung infection which must have completely resolved.

It was the suddenness of unexpected gratitude which surprised us the most. One is able to understand such instances only when one considers the view of a patient. The patient is in distress, howsoever large or small the cause may be. A solution comes like a ray of light at the end of a long dark tunnel. When the god-sent gift comes with a smile, one then realizes that the situation is not as bad as it seemed. Once again, one becomes the master of the game.

One also relishes the appreciation one gets from a patient who gets well with or even without, *sometimes in spite of* your treatment. The expression of gratitude may differ from one patient to the other, but the feelings conveyed remain the same. Smaller and subtle expressions are even more pleasant!

A cardio-thoracic surgeon, who had been my senior colleague at the institute, once narrated the story of a '*chaat-wala*' who was operated upon by him in the past. The '*chaat-wala*' not only refused to charge for the 'delicacy' he served in the '*rehri market*' to the surgeon, but used to offer discount to the whole staff from the surgeon's department whenever someone happened to visit the place. The surgeon colleague had never gone back to him to avoid embarrassment.

29.

BARRIERS

I have been always envious of pediatricians for their patience while dealing with children, especially the tiny tots. Only they can effectively communicate with them. Of course parents constitute an exception. They are blessed with extra ordinary talents to handle their own children. Pediatricians seem to have magic wands in their hands. It is a yeoman job to work with the little gods who are not in the best of their health. The inhospitable surroundings of a hospital are enough to spoil the mood of adults let alone small kids. I have always felt edgy whenever I had to handle a sick child even though on a rare occasion. Most of the times, I would refer the child to a pediatrician.

The situation was different in case of senior citizens. A large number of my patients belonged to that category. One needed skills almost similar to or better than those of a pediatrician for management of the elderly. The situation was compounded further in case of the grand seniors in the last decade before they completed a full century. I had my toughest test of perseverance with Mr. Sondhi who had visited me for his "weakening lungs". It is commonly said one reverts to childhood in older age. It was for the first time that I personally experienced the truth of the saying.

Mr Sondhi was a tall individual of thin build who was fairly healthy. He came walking to my office without the need for any support. Neither he, nor his attendant could exactly tell me his age in years. Someone at the Registration Desk had filled the column with the figure of ninety two. Incidentally, his hearing was not as well preserved as the rest of his faculties.

The conversation between the two of us had gone on for a fairly long time without any meaningful conclusion.

"Mr. Sondhi, what made you to come to the hospital? What are your problems?" I asked.

"I am sorry that I have barged in. You see that I am an old man. I retired from the Government service several years ago", he replied.

"That must have been a wonderful experience. It was a long inning for you to serve. I am sorry to be brief because of the paucity of time. How can I help you now? What are your symptoms?" I asked again.

"I have a son who works in Chennai and a daughter in Mumbai. Both are married but live far away from here", he said.

"That is quite usual with most of the families these days. Children have their own jobs and families to look after", I tried to rationalize. To bring him to the main issue, I again made a direct inquiry: "But what about your health? How well do you keep yourself?"

"I do go for a morning walk in the park. Sometimes I also go to the market with this boy Babu. He is an excellent helper. I pay him well for his work. God bless him for his service to me".

"Yes Sir….what about…." I tried to ask for his symptoms once more.

"He is very helpful. I pay him well. He has come from the hills and lives with me in the same house. I shall not ever like to lose him."

I kept quiet and allowed him to continue with his story.

"You see, he also cooks food for me. My wife is long dead. She was a very nice cook. I did not ever bother for any other help till she was there. She took care of all my needs all the time". He was getting a bit emotional. I kept listening.

"She had diabetes. But she was very fond of eating. She would not take care of her diet in spite of the advice of her doctor".

I tried to sympathize, "It is always difficult to stick to rigid dietary restrictions. You need to take medicine to control your blood sugar levels.

"I have now come to this hospital for my weakening lungs and heart. I decided to seek a medical opinion before it is too late for a cure". He finally seemed to come to the point. But my hopes were dashed when he started talking about his past experiences while in service. He had meritoriously served as a revenue officer for several decades.

"I was an officer in Jind State during British rule. With great difficulty, I got my allotment to Punjab after partition….." I tried to interrupt him with my medical questioning. He did not seem to listen. "A long service has weakened my lungs. I served with dignity and honour. There was no corruption then. Those were the days when…."

He kept going on and on for well over twenty minutes. Meanwhile Babu mentioned that his master is a bit hard of hearing. I had been trying to shout myself to help communication. My attempt to put questions in writing was not successful at all. He would try to read but go on with his own monologue. "Our standards have in fact gone down after independence. There is corruption everywhere……."

The people sitting outside in the waiting hall were getting restless. The pitch of our voices was possibly adding to their frustration. Several of them were repeatedly trying to open the door to intrude into the room. It seemed that a mutiny might ensue if the interview continued in the same fashion. I again looked up to Babu to somehow make his boss understand. He himself was clueless but equally anxious to leave. "Sir, you please give the treatment. *Sahib* will go on like this. I will make him understand at home."

That seemed like wise advice. In the absence of an apparent indication, I wrote a rather nonspecific prescription. I explained the details to Babu, who was now quite relaxed. He carefully took Mr. Sondhi by the arm and nodded to the exit. I did not wish to offend Mr. Sondhi. But my fears were misplaced. Mr. Sondhi was neither disturbed nor perturbed. Most gracefully, he rose to leave. He was very happy to be seen by a doctor. He gleefully thanked for the medical help he had received. Before going out he promised to see me again. "Sir, I am obliged that you took care of me. I shall come after I finish with the medicine you have given."

"Your health is excellent. You do not need any drug. Please enjoy your walks. You shall not need a follow up visit in less than a year". He hardly seemed to care for my advice. I was trying to assure myself.

Since that time, my respect for the geriatric physicians has grown as equal to that for the pediatricians. It is a daunting task to understand the sufferings of all those disadvantaged people, who are either unable to express themselves or whom we are unable to understand. Blessed are the physicians who can break the barriers.

30.

THE BIG LEAGUE

Ms. Sood was a young officer of the Indian Administrative Services who fell ill with fever. She had been known to be asthmatic since her childhood. She was admitted in the private ward of the hospital under a general medicine unit. No firm diagnosis had been made and a number of investigations done thus far were inconclusive. She had been administered various antibiotics without any significant benefit. I was called for consultation when she developed cough as a diagnosis of complicated pneumonia was suspected.

Surprisingly, she remained aloof when I along with my senior resident went to see her. I tried to introduce myself, but she hardly showed an interest. "Doctor, please do not ask me to repeat all what I have told a number of your doctors in the hospital. I am quite tired. I had a lousy break-fast in the morning. Moreover, the room is so untidy", she showered me with several of her complaints. "It is difficult for me to go through the same set of questions each time. It is so boring". I was stunned but tried to seek her cooperation, "Madame, I am sorry for the condition of the room. I shall let the medical superintendent know of your complaints about the room. Please tell me something about your medical condition to enable me to find some solution."

"What solution? So many doctors have already failed to find a diagnosis. Why don't you go through the records? Every bit must be there in the file." She was quite reluctant to part with any information. She seemed a bit tough to handle. I had already gone through the notes scribbled by various resident doctors. As usual, those were rather sketchy. I needed first-hand information. I left the room with a concise message: "I shall come later in the evening. Please rest until then." She was obviously annoyed but did not respond.

In the evening I learnt that she had left the hospital without even informing the concerned medical team. The medical consultant was not happy at the turn of events. I was also upset at her behaviour but took the incident in stride. Good riddance perhaps? But I was sure that the matter had not ended. I also expected some further fire-balls. Surprisingly, there was no follow-up bitterness.

After a few days, I got a call from the chief-secretary of the state where she was posted. I was however relaxed since I knew him very well. He was an excellent individual with a razor sharp mind. He used to visit me occasionally for his off and on attacks of asthma. Only a few months earlier, he himself had been admitted for a few days in the same ward. He was therefore quite familiar with the conditions which prevailed there.

The chief was quite direct in his approach: "Doctor Jindal, why don't you take Ms. Sood in the hospital? Her condition does not look very bright to me". I tried to explain what had happened a few days earlier when he cut me short:

"I know she has always been a little arrogant. Please do not bother about what she says. She needs immediate medical attention. Her father is rather scared about her health." I heaved a sigh of relief. Apparently, there was no serious deterioration. I had no real qualms about her readmission. She deserved this concession for her sickness.

In the hospital, she did not make any mention of her previous hospitalization or why she had left. I as well did not rub any salt in that wound! She did give her medical history as required by us. There were obvious changes in her x-ray findings which along with further investigations helped us make a clear diagnosis. She responded well to the treatment which was given. At discharge, she did say that she should have started her treatment earlier. I only smiled.

Such attitude problems were related to the false ego nurtured by some people who felt proud being titled as 'important' or 'very important person'. I learnt in my early training period that the importance of a person in social circles is a relative attribute. Moreover, importance of a person is neither permanent nor universal. A *panchayat sarpanch* is quite a VIP for residents of a village, but not for people in a larger city. In the hospital, there existed an official hierarchical protocol for the VIPs visiting the doctors' offices for consultation or admissions. In a status-conscious society, a lot of people with different backgrounds with an official or social position did not like to wait. Celebrities of different categories constituted a similar group of VIPs. Illness of such an individual did cause a bit of discomfort in our minds.

Incidentally, there was no dearth of VIPs in Chandigarh who belonged to the big league. Besides its own administrative machinery governed by the Central Government, Chandigarh had the distinction of housing two governments of the states of Punjab and Haryana. Consequently, there were two governors, two chief-ministers and a host of ministers and officials of Punjab and Haryana residing in the city. The VIPs of Himachal Pradesh and sometimes from Jammu & Kashmir also preferred the Institute at Chandigarh for their illnesses. Fortunately, there was only one High Court with no such stately division between the judges. Delhi of course had a much larger share of important people than Chandigarh. But Delhi was too big for any comparison.

It was not entirely unusual for some privileged people to avail free treatment as a matter of right. Occasionally, a comical situation would develop in a case of an arrogant attitude of such an individual. I could never forget an incidence which happened several years earlier during the days of my residency. A senior officer who had recently retired from a government job was going through investigations for his problems. I, as a junior resident, had drawn his blood sample. I was supposed to send that sample to the biochemistry and hematology laboratories. Certain payments were required to be made for the tests. I asked the concerned individual to do so at the fee-counter on the ground floor of the hospital. He was taken aback. "Are you joking in asking me to make the payments? I have helped this Institute with numerous favours during my service. None has ever asked me to pay for the simple tests" he was almost furious in his response. I politely said that I could not help. There was no mechanism with which I could get the charges waived off on my own. As per procedure, he had to pay and later submit the bills to his office for reimbursement.

It was not possible to get him to agree to follow the procedure. I was irritated at his insistence but could not show it openly. I decided to get the tests done as 'poor-free', wrote 'Indigent' on the requisition slips. That was an alternate method which we residents sometimes adopted to short-cut the procedure. That enraged him even more. "Do I look indigent to you? I am a respectable citizen of this city" he continued to shout.

My mood was quite upset but I did not wish to enter into an argument. In those days, I was a bit too junior in the Institute hierarchy. He immediately left the place and went to the Office of the Director. I do not know what conspired between the two of them. After some time, an attendant from the office of the Director came to fetch the blood samples. I did not see the gentleman ever again. The Director, Dr. Chhuttani was too polished and cultured in his behaviour. He never mentioned the incident to me. He was his usual-self on the rounds the next day.

It is always difficult to provide a good medical opinion to a VIP in the general outpatient clinic. The chaos created due to the presence of a large body of subordinates and/or well-wishers disturbs the routine schedule of the out-patient clinic. Therefore, other patients who are waiting in the queue, sometimes for hours together, resent their presence.

Heated arguments and even minor skirmishes were not uncommon between the attendants of visiting VIPs and the Institute staff. The boys operating the lifts and the security men at the gates were particularly troubled. Inquiries for identification would generally upset people visiting doctors or their relatives admitted in the wards. I remember a Member of Parliament accompanied by a gunman who wanted to enter the elevator to go upstairs. When requested by the lift operator to identify himself, the honourable member felt furious. "I am not used to this type of behaviour from people like you".

He used all kinds of abusive accusations threatening to get him suspended. I had been waiting for the elevator to move. I found it hard to convince or pacify his temper. The lift-operator had little alternative but to let him in. The incident led me to recall a story of the past told to me in my childhood that a Maharaja of Patiala was once refused entry into his palace at night when he went back incognito. The Maharaja, forced to stay outside his palace, rewarded the guard for his exemplary sincerity and diligence of duty the next morning.

In spite of some unpleasant experiences which could possibly have been avoided, it was remarkable to see that a large number of these men would patiently wait and accept the existing arrangements, which were not very friendly in view of the several constraints which we faced. I admiringly remember that most civil and police officers, High Court judges, eminent lawyers, professors and other important people would quietly identify themselves at the gate.

With reference to the VIP culture I would like to cite an instance of *overkill* by those who look after them. A senior minister of the government of India had gone to the Himachal hills for some official engagement. On his way back to Delhi by road on a Sunday morning, he decided to see me at the Institute for a medical problem which had been there for some time. My car was stopped at the gate by the police when I went to meet the minister in the hospital. "You cannot enter the hospital; a *'toap'* (a big gun) is in", I was told. It was difficult to convince the police about the purpose of my visit. Cell phones were not there. It was after quite some time that an officer of the Institute Security came looking and rescued me from a potential detainment. Unaware of the developments, the minister patiently waited for me. I had nothing to complain about the matter.

I had a few opportunities to temporarily receive a VIP tag myself whenever I was required to visit a governor or a chief minister. The condition became most difficult for me during the visit of the then Prime Minister, S. Manmohan Singh who was invited to our institute for the inauguration of Punjab-PGI tele-medicine link. As Professor-in-charge of Telemedicine, I was supposed to attend upon him during the function. Though the duty was not onerous, I was made uncomfortable by the accompanying police-escort who shadowed me the whole day. I felt immensely relieved when the ceremonies were over.

I have already dwelt upon my hurricane visit to Nepal. That was well matched by another similar trip which was perhaps even faster. I was having lunch one fine day when I was called upon to proceed to Chennai to see a senior politician admitted in the Intensive Care Unit of a local Medical College. The Jet flight from Chandigarh was due to leave for Delhi in an hour or less. I truthfully expressed my inability to organize an urgent booking like the one desired in the given time period. However, at the other end, things happened and I got a call from the airport in the next fifteen minutes that they were waiting for me to board. In fact it took me relatively longer to arrange to reach the airport. I finally managed to land in Chennai well after dinner time late at night.

Unfortunately, the patient was seriously ill and already on full life- support. There was little which could be done. Two other colleagues, one each from Mumbai and Hyderabad, besides those from Chennai were also there. Our joint consultation probably helped to assuage the family as well as assure the local treatment team that the best had been done. We had a frank discussion with the family who were quite well informed of the outcome. I thought my trip was futile. Perhaps it was not so. I realized the value of my visit when I received a letter of immense gratitude on behalf of the highly satisfied family.

31.

HOLY WATER – THE LAST WISH

(Adapted from the original story of the author "Holy Water – The Last Wish" published in "Final Days: Stories at the End of Life" with permission of the publishers, American College of Chest Physicians, Chicago, USA 2003).

The Ganges is considered to be a sacred river by the Hindus and worshipped as *'the Mother'* since millennia. It is personified as the goddess Ganga who reflects prosperity. Taking a bath in the Ganges is a dream cherished by each Hindu to wash away the sins of a lifetime. Traditionally, it is almost imperative for Hindus to immerse the ashes of their dead kin into the Ganges. The death rites remain incomplete until this final step is dutifully performed. Immersion in the Ganges liberates all from the cycle of life and death.

A mythological story relates the descent of Ganga from the Heavens to the Earth in response to the prayers of *King Bhagiratha*. He wished Ganga to wash away the ashes of his former kin who had been wandering as ghosts on Earth. Their final rites could not be performed after they were reduced to ashes by the fiery sight of the angry sage Kapila. Ganga became furious when ordered by Lord Shiva to go to the Earth. She descended with a great fury and force.

It was again Lord Shiva who let her fall on His head and arrested her in His long locks of hair. She was released only after prayers and promises to stay calm. The story goes on that ever after, She remained on earth to bring prosperity to human beings.

The Ganges takes its origin from the breath-taking glacier Gaumukh (Cow's Mouth) located in greater Himalayan range near the picturesque Gangotri town in Uttrakhand state. It flows down through most of northern India to merge with the Bay of Bengal in the East. Being the major source of water for fields along its course, it forms the primary life line for farmers. Its water is considered as nectar or ambrosia – the food of the gods. It is because of this sanctity that every Hindu likes to drink the ambrosia before he dies. It is also used during holy festivals and functions including marriages and child-births.

I myself have grown up listening to the sanctity and marvels of the water of the Ganges. Several of my family members have deep faith and love for the Ganges and the sacred cities of Rishikesh and Haridwar through which it flows. I have enjoyed the inspiring beauty and serenity of the Ganges many times during my vacations. All along, I had known of its importance and place in the Hindu psyche. But I realized the depth of conviction amongst devotees much later when I was confronted by one of my patients near the end of his life. It was several years ago when I was faced with this issue in my professional practice.

A pious and humble man, Ram Avatar was a staunch believer in God and an honest Brahmin. All alone, he lived in a local temple and worked as a priest. I occasionally used to meet him when I went to the nearby temple for religious ceremonies. He had no children, his wife was long dead. He had smoked cigarettes for several years, suffered from advanced obstructive lung disease and chronic respiratory failure. He had been in and out of the hospital several times in the past. Every time he was discharged out of the hospital, he used to laugh away: "The reprieve is temporary. I promise to see you soon."

During one of his visits he had the premonition of death. He wanted a change in medicine but did not wish for admission. Not hopeful of recovery, he was adamant in his refusal. I on the other hand, wanted his immediate admission. He was in obvious need of *mechanical respiratory assistance.* He was yet in command of his senses, and was able to over-rule the pleas and arguments of all of us.

Ram Avatar did not agree for admission; he was skeptical about the fulfilment of his last wish in the hospital. He was familiar with the standard hospital practices, of the unattached and unemotional behaviour of hospital personnel, though he appreciated the excellent medical care and the efforts made by the staff to save the life of a sick patient. Ram Avatar was sure he was dying. All through his life, he had performed customary *havan and puja* for others. He did not wish to die sans prayers and rituals. He used to repeatedly argue: "We all take care of ceremonies and prayers for the living. We perform all kinds of rituals for the dead. What about the sensitive moments of death? A dying person is the most neglected being in our society. He is left to the mercy of others."

He was sure that the medical personnel were not trained to deal with the spiritual needs of patients close to death. I was confronted with a difficult question. Undoubtedly, there is perceptible lack of sensitivity to death during the last moments of life in large hospitals and institutions. There is no place for *non-medical measures*, apparently considered as futile in the strict scientific protocols and guidelines for treatment, before or after the death. The family members and the priests, who need to take care, are not supposed to be present in hospital wards and intensive care units.

It was with some effort that I came to know of his last wish. He wished to have the sacred water of the Ganges as the last drink of his life. It was a rather simple wish which was a standard practice adopted for a person dying at home. Not infrequently, the holy water is poured into the mouth during the last gasps of a dying person. Yet, it would be conveniently overlooked in a busy hospital. I was not sure myself whether the wish could be genuinely attended to in my ward.

I sat with him and initiated a dialogue in praise of the Ganges. Within a few minutes, he opened up and started narration of the mythological story of the Ganges. He endlessly talked of the ever affectionate Mother Ganges and Her holy water which washes off all sins. He described the panorama of green fields and crowded cities through which it flows. "It serves humankind since after the release from Lord Shiva's locks of hair" he repeatedly impressed upon me. He felt comfortable after I patiently listened to him. He agreed only after I promised to keep the Holy water by his side and personally ensure that his wish was respected by the staff on duty. There was no difficulty in getting the holy water. Most of the devout Hindus stored the water of the Ganges in containers at home. He offered blessings for me.

The Ganges water, available in his own home, was brought and kept by his bedside.

After admission, his condition deteriorated. He required mechanical respiratory support the very next day. All through his stay in the Intensive Care Unit, I was anxious whether the staff would live up to expectations. Unfortunately, there was no close relative with him who could take the responsibility in his/her own hands. He had always lived in the temple amongst a lot of gods and devotees. Yet it seemed he was all alone near the time of his death.

Contrary to the expectations of most of us, he responded very well to therapy. Once again, there was a great sense of satisfaction for the medical team. Every one of us including myself felt rewarded when he was discharged from the ward after about a week. He was back to his work in the temple at the feet of his gods.

I did pay him a visit once or twice afterwards in the temple. He was somehow managing his work. He always gave me special *Prasad* of the tasteful Indian *burfi* or some other sweet whenever I visited. It was about three months later that I came to know of his sudden death at home within the premises of the temple. He could not be brought to the hospital. His end came in divine company listening to religious chants. I was sure that he must be listening to the soft music of the ripples of Mother Ganges during his last moments. The junior priest by his bedside had told me that he was very calm and fully satisfied near his death. The priest assured me that the Ganges water was indeed poured in his mouth when he collapsed.

32.

ONE MORE WORLD TO GO

Deepak Sharma was a perfect gentleman who taught at a local college. He consulted me since he was bothered with distressing cough for a few weeks. He had tried different cough syrups without any benefit. On further investigations, he was detected to suffer from cancer of lung with an aggressive progression. Different modalities of treatment were administered without much success. Soon, the cancer was widely spread for which he opted against any further curative treatments. Thereafter, we resorted to a palliative approach for relief of his symptoms. It seemed obvious that he had only a few more weeks, or at best two to three months to live.

I always found him pleasing whenever I visited him either in the hospital ward or at his home. He never lost the smile on the face. One day, I dared to ask him if he was bothered about his death. He replied with a great degree of content: "No. I have greatly enjoyed my life with my students and my family. Now, I have one more world to go"! I was quite satisfied myself and patted his back. I was sure that he would continue to teach wherever he went. That meeting furthered my interest in issues related to end-of-life care of terminally ill patients.

Deepak reminded me of Roger Bone, an American physician who pioneered intensive care for critically sick patients. Throughout his life, he had provided artificial respiratory support to hundreds of his patients. Some of his papers published in the professional journals are cited whenever one discusses the issue of critical care. But more than his contribution to the subject of critical care, he is remembered for his fight with death and his friendship with life. "Life had been good to me" he surmised. Factually, he had been good to life. He became an epitome of a good life after his death.

I have always valued the excellent 'pieces of mind' which he wrote about his life before his death in 1997 at the young age of 56 years. The two small pieces**, which he wrote underlined the importance which he gave to trivia in life. He enjoyed trivia, had commented that the seemingly ordinary things become important over time more than the otherwise seemingly bigger achievements. What Mirza Ghalib would seek from his Urdu couplets or Wordsworth from daffodils, was discovered by Roger Bone in the taste of lemonade on a summer afternoon. He died soon afterwards while relishing another taste of lemonade. It was his wife who offered him lemonade when she first came to know of his illness. "Suddenly the lemonade became the point," Bone said. "I tasted the sweetness of the drink, and though I felt my life passing before me I tried to savour the moment."

** *'The Taste of Lemonade in a Summer Afternoon' and 'Another Taste of Lemonade', Journal of American Medical Association, Vols. 273 and 274, 1995.*

I had met Dr. Bone at an Annual Conference of the American College of Chest Physicians in America. The first and only meeting left a lasting impression. There was quite an informal atmosphere at the inaugural dinner of the College. He was not only friendly in approach but also showed a great degree of enthusiasm. He profusely talked on different issues in medicine. He did not let me feel that he was ill. He nodded with a smile at my invitation for him to come to India but did not give an affirmative reply. Generally speaking, Americans have been warm in response to an invitation. Perhaps he knew that the visit would never happen but did not like to verbalize his inability. Perhaps he did not wish to say no to an invitation.

I was greatly honoured for my selection as one of the recipients of the Commendation Award of the American Chest Foundation for End of Life Care. The award was instituted by the family of Dr Bone, after his death. This also provided me with an opportunity to meet his wife Rosemary and his lovely daughter Mary Katherine when I received the award. Both of them were as warm as Dr. Bone himself.

Deepak died after about a month of my last visit. I could read plenty in what he had said and practiced. Like Roger Bone, Deepak talked of the need to possess good health to enjoy the gifts granted by God. For him, the smell of roses, the chirping of birds and the soft purr of the flow of wind- all the precious things were as enjoyable as teaching a student. A look at the star-studded sky on a dark night, the bright sun shine on a cold morning or a rainbow after a heavy rain fall, all provide an immense amount of pleasure.

One only needs to appreciate the riches which have been bestowed by God.

One is often burdened with unnecessary stresses worrying about things which one does not have. Unfortunately, we overlook or ignore the free gifts of nature which we have in plenty. Good health is the most precious commodity which one possesses. A healthy human being is a very rich person endowed with immense wealth. Material wealth is of far less importance in the absence of good physical and mental health. A balance of joy and happiness with a good and healthy life is all that is meaningful.

But can we ensure or insure good health all the time? That is perhaps not possible. Health does deteriorate with time. Also, death is inevitable, which we all know since time immemorial. Every time, one needs to learn from the famous story of "The Enchanted Pool" in that great Hindu epic - the *Mahabharta*. During their exile, while wandering in the jungles from one place to another, the five *Pandava brothers* were exhausted. They finally found a pond of water which in fact was a magic creation of a *Yaksha* who was *Yama,* the lord of death. One by one, all the four younger brothers of *Yudhishtra* tried to draw water from the pool to quench their thirst. They all fell dead after ignoring the warning of the *Yaksha*; they attempted to draw water from the pool without taking care to answer the questions posed by him. It was *Yudhishtra* who kept his cool and agreed to the *Yaksha's* demands. After a series of questions, the *Yaksha* finally wanted to know "what is the strangest thing in the world?" The unfazed *Yudhishtra* replied: "we see everyone in this world dying one day and yet we keep on believing that we shall live forever". Satisfied with his replies, the *Yaksha* granted back life to all the *Pandava brothers* who carried on with their journey.

Sometime ago, I came across a short story told by a patient. It goes on that a mortal human being had pleased *Yama*, with his fearlessness. He was not afraid of the Lord of death who therefore decided to grant him a boon. The man was quite modest in his wish- "Oh Lord. You are the final king of salvation. You may come to take me back from this world whenever my time has come. Please give me adequate time to prepare for the departure. I should be warned of my death before you decide to come." Many years later, *Yama* arrived at the doors of his house one day. The man was stunned to find the unexpected guest, reminded *Yama* about the promise he had made in the past. The Death-god politely replied: "Oh, you ignorant man, I had given you plenty of warnings in the past two decades since we met. Your hairs were greyed; cataract produced in your eyes; your joints made painful; your arteries narrowed and so on. Every time, you defeated me by voiding the warning signals – you dyed your hair, repaired your cataract, replaced your joints, stented your arteries, and so on. Every time I had to postpone my visit. I was left with no option now. I had to finally come."

Marvellously, man has purchased health as well as delayed death. He has achieved a partial technological invincibility in the struggle for life. But do we find immortal people from the past? The peace of mind seems to have been lost somewhere in this complex conglomeration. Peace somehow has no direct relation with technological superiority, money, power, achievement, intelligence, or even with prayers and worship. I believe that the most successful method to achieve peace is the acceptance of happiness and misery, success and failure and of disease and death. It is the present which gives us hope for life in the future.

Several times, I have tried to dwell upon meanings of what Deepak had said. I know that he did not believe in the re-birth theory. But he was firmly convinced that the death is not the end of one's life. One lives beyond that point. Undoubtedly, he lived in the hearts of his students and numerous other followers. Deepak had imparted training to a large number of his students who had gone through his classes in the past three decades. They greatly admired his gift of education.

Deepak never felt defeated. Even the terminal part of his life had turned into a crucial lesson. That is what Roger Bone also tried to tell. He had given life to a large number of patients in intensive care units. His work had helped to improve the care of patients with *sepsis*. He loved life but did not wish to live morbidly for the very little time he was left with. He wished to die at home without an artificial prolongation of the process of his death. He knew that he had reached the end of the road. His life constituted a real-time example of lessons in end-of-life care. He wrote: "Doctors want to cure, to think that for every diagnosis there is a prescription to make things better. But what do you do when the cure is a failure? You may walk away. Doctors need a way to deal with failure..."

One may keep on searching for one's enemy. What or who is the greatest enemy of mental peace? Is it poverty? Ill health? Jealousy? Competition? Depression? Helplessness? Fear of Failure? Disease? or fear of death? We do not know the answer. One can however learn a lesson from Deepak.

Seek pleasure in the commonplace events of life. How relieving it is to find a place to park your car in a jammed parking place or to find a seat in a crowded bus. Equally enjoyable is the thankful smile of a client or the sense of gratitude shown by a patient. The blooming of flowers, a pensive morning walk, the sight of magnificent hills, a flight of pigeons or the taste of a lemonade – all can provide immense pleasure only if we are ready to perceive. Factually speaking, the seemingly trivial things do not become more important over time – they remain important all the time.

One More Life to Live – Last prayer of a sick man

Beyond the earth's confines,
with the stars in the sky.
Above the oceans in the clouds
my hopes fly.

    In my bed I lie,
    with an illness severe.
    I have less to live,
    my doctors fear.

When the pins prick,
and the ants creep on legs.
When the stomach aches,
and the body pains.

    When the mouth is sore,
    and the eyes pour.
    When the truth is scary,
    and the lies don't work.

When the hopes fade,
and the needles fail.
Your touch does the magic,
and your words prevail.
> Don't tell me lies,
> there is little scope.
> I may not live long,
> but give me some hope.

You are good to me,
to thee I pray.
My hopes are my treasury,
don't take away.
> In my sleep I dream,
> of things very beautiful.
> Give me more next time,
> I pray to the Merciful.

My life has been full,
I had plenty to give.
There is one more world to go,
there is one more life to live.

33.

DILEMMA OF CRITICAL CARE

"Doctor Jindal, when should I expect my mother to breathe by herself? It is extremely painful to see her suffer in this condition". Mr. Yadav had asked me that question many times in the past several days. Unfortunately, I could not add any more to my reply "it is hard to say" which was too familiar to him. It was true that I did not know the answer to his question. We were doing all what was possible, but we did not have any hope. Mr. Yadav and his family knew it too.

It was more than two months since Mrs. Janaki was admitted in the Intensive Care Unit of the hospital. She was deeply comatose, provided with artificial respiratory support with the help of a mechanical device – the ventilator. Her heart was beating still and her brain activity was also present. So we did not have any alternate option but to wait and watch. Only God could decide the future and only time could end the misery.

Mrs. Janaki was apparently healthy when she suffered a sudden stroke. She had lapsed into unconsciousness due to a massive brain hemorrhage. In a desperate attempt at resuscitation, she was put on a mechanical ventilator.

However, even after two months of treatment, there was not even a tinge of recovery. She had remained in an unconscious state ever since the first day. Obviously, everyone in the family was getting impatient.

Mr. Yadav was a resourceful man. He reminded me again and again that money was not a problem at all. He could buy any medicine or purchase the services of any doctor if it was going to help her mother. He could spend as much as was needed. He kept on requesting repeatedly: "Please get her out of the woods." But the scope of treatment was rather limited. No magic drug could get her out of that state. The role of surgery had already been ruled out.

Tired of prolonged hospitalization, Mr. Yadav suggested to me in frustration: "Why not let her die peacefully? It has become impossible for us to wait any further in the absence of a chance of recovery." By then, I knew that the question would come sooner than later. I was curious myself as to how to 'let her die peacefully'. Just to test the depth of his thoughts, I told him the options practiced in countries elsewhere in the world - "We can either withdraw the respiratory support or stop her feeds. Which one of the option do you think can be considered?"

He got immediately cautious. "There is no question of stopping feeds. Can we discontinue the ventilator and take her home?"

"It is most unlikely. In all probabilities, she will collapse the moment we stop the ventilator", I replied.

I knew that the answer was going to be 'no'. It was not possible to take the onus of 'allowing the death' of one's mother. How could he accept that responsibility? "I shall discuss it further with other family members", he said.

There was no further discussion. Mr. Yadav's visits to the hospital were reduced thereafter. The issue remained alive but the status quo prevailed for several more weeks until the patient passed away due to multiple complications. I repeatedly tried to ponder over the dilemma. I could have perhaps persuaded him to make that decision. But should I have done that? I do not think so. As a doctor, I could not decide on behalf of the family. In critical care, one continues to face that issue almost every day.

Sardara Singh met the same fate as Mrs. Janaki but for the fact that he remained conscious throughout his stay in the Intensive Care Unit. He was a middle aged individual who had been hale and hearty before his illness. One fine day, he developed some fever followed by weakness of both of his legs with in a period of a few hours. He was rushed to the hospital where neurological examination revealed the presence of paraplegia. A diagnosis of Gullain Barre Syndrome was made and treatment instituted as necessary.

Gullain Barre Syndrome is a disease of uncertain cause but commonly follows a viral infection. It is named after Gullain, Barre and Strohl who diagnosed the illness in two soldiers in 1916. However, the clinical picture was actually described long before by a French physician Landry in 1859. To give appropriate credit to all the discoverers, some people like to call the disease as Landry Gullain Barre Strohl Syndrome. A series of patients were reported in 1970 following administration of swine flu vaccination. Post vaccination GB syndrome remains a dreadful, though extremely rare complication of a viral vaccine. The syndrome may manifest with different neurological features of which respiratory paralysis is the most serious. In most cases, the condition is curable and muscle weakness reversible.

By the early morning of next day, Sardara Singh showed progression of weakness of limbs along with involvement of muscles of the upper trunk. Worst of all, he started complaining of breathing difficulty which became distressing very soon. He expressed an extreme sense of suffocation as if he was being throttled. He was soon intubated and started on mechanical ventilation. He felt better almost immediately afterwards. Everybody heaved a sigh of relief and hoped that he would be weaned off the ventilator in the next couple of days.

Unfortunately, the recovery from the illness did not happen. There was no improvement in his respiratory or limb muscle weakness. He could neither move his limbs nor breathe on his own. We attempted weaning from ventilation several times but failed. Whenever we tried to reduce the ventilatory support, he became uncomfortable, demanding to urgently restore the support. In other words, he was totally ventilator-dependent.

The family had a limited income which got further reduced due to illness of the head of the family. In spite of the highly subsidized costs at the government hospital, they could not purchase the daily requirement of drugs and disposables. Provision of a support ventilator at home was perhaps the only alternative. Cost would have been highly prohibitive at any private hospital. We remained in a quandary for a fairly long period. Sardara Singh's wife along with her son was always there at his bed side. Others kept on checking off and on. She used to plead every day to do something. What could I do? I tried to get some financial help through different agencies to get a domiciliary ventilator. However, the family members were too afraid to operate a sophisticated machine at home. Additionally, they were not ready to leave the hospital hoping every day that he would walk out on his feet.

In between, Sardara Singh developed hospital-acquired infection which was treated with administration of costly antibiotics. A few other complications were also managed with one or the other treatment. Every day on the rounds, I used to say hello to him. I could not directly communicate with him about his illness. Yet I could understand what he used to say everyday with his open eyes – "Doctor, give some wonder drug. I wish to breathe." I had nothing to offer.

Finally, he succumbed to his illness following a massive bleed from his lungs. I got the news from my resident while going to attend a meeting for purchase of more ventilators for the department. I am not sure if I felt aggrieved or relieved at his liberation. Probably, it was a mixture of both feelings. There was no regret; we had done what was required to be done.

Both Mrs. Janaki and Sardara Singh were two among hundreds of others who were provided with assisted respiration in my department. Both together constituted a bad example where ventilation got prolonged beyond a reasonable time. There was no hope for Mrs. Janaki from the very beginning. Having been diagnosed with a massive brain hemorrhage, one could have possibly avoided the initiation of respiratory support. It would have been extremely risky to take that bold step in a hospital where facilities were available. Sardara Singh could have survived and lived a meaningful though dependent life in bed at home if his family resources were adequate. None had any control over their situation.

It is common for me as well others in the team to face situations of terminal care. It is always a complex issue to look after patients near death. I faced innumerable dilemmas of decision-making most importantly the need to continue the treatment. There are conditions when most of the drugs and other treatments being given to a patient with an end-stage disease are not just futile but extremely painful. To face a patient in distress has never been easy. I have always felt that to leave a patient to his fate in distress is as illogical and immoral as to discontinue. But more often than not, the mere thought of discontinuation has shaken consciences. Factually, the Indian Supreme Court has given more than one judgment against discontinuation.

It had been most difficult when the choice was left to me to decide at my own discretion. That had been particularly so when I had to decide on the issue myself in case of my own near and dear. I had to bear the trauma of great pain more than once. The stress was several folds more in the case of my two sisters who were admitted in terminal stages under my charge at different times in the Respiratory Intensive Care Unit. The trauma persisted for much longer that I would have expected. It was remarkable that both of them had willed their eyes for donation after their deaths. The issue of end-of-life care also encouraged me to take a lead in developing guidelines for withdrawal of assisted respiratory supports at my institute.

Patients on ventilatory assistance always suffered from life-threatening conditions, though not necessarily from terminal illnesses. We had a larger number of patients who were successfully weaned and sent home. Besides a few earlier stories told in this collection, I remember Ram Sewak who was found gasping by his wife in the early morning in his hut in a field. Both of them along with their children were sleeping on the floor. He was suspected to have been bitten by a poisonous snake even though a visible fang mark could not be found. Besides the administration of anti-snake venom, he required assisted respiratory support. Within the next forty-eight hours, Ram Sewak was comfortably sitting in his bed without any assistance. Snake bite cases made exceptional recovery in most instances provided the treatment became available in time.

Same was true for an occasional patient of respiratory arrest following a severe drug reaction. Chander Mohan, an employee of the Institute had a miraculous recovery similar to Ram Sewak. He was a patient known to have chronic asthma who worsened intermittently. He had severe pain in his back while working in a ward. He took a tablet of a pain-reliever and continued with his work. He suddenly collapsed after a few minutes with non-recordable blood pressure and fast respiration. Fortunately, he could be resuscitated and put on assisted respiration. It was largely because of his aggravated asthma that ventilation was prolonged to over 48 hours.

The history of assisted ventilation is ancient, with various attempts being documented over the centuries. It has been repeatedly mentioned that artificial life was infused back into the mouth of a dead Shunnamite child by prophet Elisha, whose name finds mention in the Hebrew Bible, the New Testament, the Quran and the Baha'i writings. It is for this reason that 'mouth to mouth breathing' used during resuscitation is commonly called as Elisha breathing. References to the possibility of artificial respiration are thereafter available in the writings of Galen of 3rd century A.D. and Vesalius the famous Renaissance era anatomist of 16th century. The modern era of assisted ventilation started only a century ago during the first world war and the subsequent polio epidemic. In the present days, the technology of assisted respiratory support is highly advanced.

It is anticipated that the advancements in molecular pharmacology, nano-technology and stem-cell therapy may in fact replace the devices for mechanical assistance with non-invasive supports in future. Even those developments are however unlikely to resolve the day to day dilemmas faced by physicians and other doctors engaged in critical care. Each new technological development is bound to create more questions and doubts about its applications and indications.

34.

KNOWLEDGE - EXPLOSION

Vijendra was one patient whom I remember with sadness. He flew from a distant place in Rajasthan along with his wife, sister Sushmita and parents to seek the *'final treatment'* at Chandigarh for his end stage lung fibrosis. He was taken to a large number of physicians at different centers all over the region in search of a treatment. The whole family including Vijendra, was tired of moving from place to place in the absence of any health benefit. They had now resolved among themselves to come to Chandigarh for one final opinion. "No more hitch-hiking. We have not travelled a single mile to our destination in the last few years." These were the tired expressions of the father while narrating the history of his illness. He had been brought to the Institute with the strong recommendation of an uncle who happened to serve as a senior judge in Delhi.

Unlike the parents who had little hope, the sister and the wife were searching for a cure. The sister had thoroughly searched on the internet for different treatment modalities. The boy was a born albino. The whole family was informed about the rare combination of lung fibrosis with albinism. Unfortunately, the diagnosis could not be established in the absence of genetic tests. They had reached at the blind end of the tunnel with little hope of comfort. The boy could hardly move in bed without getting breathless. Using all their resources, they had managed to shift him by air on continuous oxygen administration for any potential experimental treatment.

It was only the second case of an extremely rare disease in India which I had seen in my career till that time. Apparently, we were confronted with a very rare Syndrome, which was more commonly described among the residents of Puerto-Rico. Though we could establish a firm diagnosis from the ultra-structural examination of his blood cells, his treatment was no different than what could be offered to anyone else in the presence of an advanced respiratory failure. The same was instituted in all fairness. The family, now satisfied with the final diagnosis decided to go back home.

There occurred a small crisis in the morning. The sister had come across a short report on the internet about a particular drug which was used for lung fibrosis in a small number of patients. It was reported to show a marginal benefit in the hands of the investigators. Sushmita was extremely excited. "Doctor, you cannot leave us in a lurch. You must save my brother at all costs. The drug is reported to cure the disease in several patients. Please help to get the drug for his treatment." The father was not amused. He had already made the travel arrangement. "Please let us go. I have suffered from similar experiences with the children in the past and lost a lot of money," he confided.

I had already gone through the report in the past and it had also been reviewed in our departmental *Journal Club* meeting. The authors had reported some improvement in the early stages of the syndrome, before deterioration of lung function had started. The youngsters were unable to appreciate the nuances of the statement, hidden in between the lines. It was difficult to argue in the matter. The issue got further complicated since the drug was not available in either the Indian or the European market. It was not an approved drug as yet. But the father had to yield to the wishes of the children and the plan of departure got postponed.

As per the internet search, the drug was being investigated in Japan for some other indication. The family was now keen to import the drug from there. My plea to the family to conserve its resources and limit their hopes only added to their determination. Efforts to procure the drug did not succeed in spite of the medical prescription provided by me. The drug was not yet approved for use. Sushmita could not reconcile with her failure. She felt extremely guilty in failing to procure the drug for her brother. Several times she had expressed her grief at the fate of her sister-in law who was destined to bear the maximal loss.

The family finally came to terms with the illness accepting the inevitability of the end which came rather soon. The boy breathed his last at the airport when he was being taken home. Later, I did come to know of the satisfactory resolution of grief amongst the family members, including the sister. They all had passed through a difficult time. But all along, they knew the outcome. Several weeks later, I received a letter from his uncle: "I am finding it difficult to choose words for conveying thanks and gratitude on behalf of myself....You had done all that was possible. We shall never forget the extreme compassion with which you treated the family".

The drug in question became available in the Indian market some 3-4 years later. It was released in 2010 without going through the mandatory clinical trials. Recommendations to wave off trials were made by several chest physicians including a colleague of mine who himself was involved in the care of Vijendra. Later, the case was cited as one of the general *irregularities* by a Parliamentary Committee investigating the functioning of the Drug Controller of India. All those nice-hearted physicians were questioned for a possible collusion with pharmaceutical companies. I myself had to defend the decision of my colleagues in a tough interview on one of the premier English Channel on National Television. Everybody was asking how a recommendation could be made for a drug which was not released in either America or Europe. Within the next few years, the drug became also available in most of the Western countries.

I have never regretted the decision of my colleagues for that recommendation. One need not unnecessarily wait for clinical trials to be done in India if adequate data are available from other credible sources. I must also accept that the drug is not revolutionary in any sense. It may provide limited benefit in a small number of patients selected on defined parameters.

I firmly believe that the confidence posed in the physician who treats, is of greater use than the most modern approaches cited on the internet. Not infrequently, a doctor may also find it hard to take a decision in the presence of conflicting evidence. He may find himself inadequately informed in the light of the information presented to him. Not infrequently, one is compelled to adopt a particular line of management on the basis of inputs from the worldwide web provided by patients and/or their families.

Vijendra's case regarding information available on internet, more precisely on Wikipedia was relatively simple. It is more complex in case of several other treatments. I can particularly cite the case of Onkar Singh with reference to the management of the same problem of lung fibrosis with lung transplantation. The discussions on issues of lung transplantation had frequently proven to be tragically comical. An experience with Shibu the son of Onkar Singh was one such example.

Shibu had read about lung transplantation as the only possible option for end stage disease of his father. He had no idea at all about transplantation – perhaps not about the respiratory system either. I am sure that he hardly knew the difference between lungs and other body organs. He was a young, care free student who rarely went outside the walls of his college cafe – more appropriately the cyber-café. The boy was addicted to surfing and chatting on the internet. The father's illness came like a bombshell posing enormous challenges. Suddenly the boy realized the responsibilities of a son. He extensively searched for treatment modalities for end stage lung disease. Rightly so, he came with the reply in lung transplantation.

"Sir, I have come to know of a remarkable treatment. I am sure that my father can live a normal life after lung transplantation". It was natural for him to seek the only curative treatment from the hospital.

"You need a lung for your father for transplantation, dear Shibu". It came to me as a sudden shock when he first put the question to me in the outpatient clinic. "Lungs are not easily available in this country," I added. Unfortunately, lung transplantation in India had not started as yet. Even today in 2015, the facility is extremely limited, largely because of the non-availability of donors.

"Cannot we procure the same from abroad"? He posed. I did not have the time to enter into a long argument in the crowded clinic. "We shall discuss it later", I decided to admit his father in the ward.

My next confrontation with him had happened on the second day of admission. As innocently as on the first day, he told me – "Sir, I am ready to donate my lungs for my father." I could hardly believe my ears. I sat with him for some time and listened to his story. He had been arguing with the residents on one or the other issue throughout the day. Fed up with his persistent queries, one of the residents commented that the lung could be transplanted if he agreed to donate the same. Without hesitation, he agreed to accept the challenge. Next day, he dutifully conveyed that he was happy to part with one of his lung. (Doctors in India have often used this trick to ask for blood donation to get rid of hang-around relatives and well-wishers crowding the wards).

That was an intemperate suggestion made by a tired resident doctor. But the boy hardly had the competence to understand the hidden satire in the doctor's comment. Lungs could not be obtained from a living donor like Shibu. (A lobe from a lung of a live-donor has been used at some of the centers particularly in Japan). I had to use a lot many explanations and examples to let him feel at ease. He was certainly more satisfied at the time of discharge of his father. I had to mildly admonish my resident doctor, though I could not blame him either. The doctors also get impatient at times.

The knowledge explosion of the last quarter of a century has caused enormous shifts in the practice of medicine. Medical information has become widely available on the internet within easy reach of every individual. The plethora of easily available information on health and disease has tremendously expanded the knowledge on options of treatment. One can find answers to a whole lot of doubts and questions with a simple click of the mouse. Diseases as well as their treatments are no more alien to lay people. Resultantly, there is a significant change in the perceptions of a large section of patients and their families towards the management plans. These are further compounded by tweets and blogs of different people in social media. The demands of patients and pressures on doctors have greatly increased. The Internet phenomenon is not just limited to the computer-savvy, modern educated class but also to lesser educated individuals from more modest backgrounds.

One would normally expect that more awareness would result in better understanding of a disease and treatment by patients. Unfortunately, online information is neither complete in itself, nor necessarily based on evidence. At the end, one develops a greater degree of anxiety than before opening the world-wide web. Someone has to critically analyze the wide range of available information to obtain the appropriate treatment. The hopes of patients get exaggerated beyond the limits of reason. Sometimes, it is the despair of prognosis which may haunt the sufferer of an incurable illness. Knowledge alone is not enough. It is difficult for an affected individual to make a wise choice. It is essential to inject wisdom into the quagmire of information.

EPILOGUE

We have entered a whole new world. There are revolutionary advances in the practice of medicine making it even more complex in the 21st century. Invasive interventions and aggressive treatments have come to occupy the centre-stage of medical management. Different kinds of surgical and genetic repairs, replacements and transplantations are being done. People wish to live long, sometimes hoping for immortality. Patients are now empowered with the knowledge of newer technologies and futuristic treatments. A new gamut of moral and ethical dilemmas have cropped up sometimes making it extremely trying to maintain a balance between what is desired and what can be offered.

Added to the dilemmas are the challenges related to conflicts which tend to assume serious proportions, not infrequently. While patients are conscious of their rights and legal protection, it is increasingly being difficult for medical fraternity to fulfil the needs and ambitions of a significant majority of patients, whether seen in a public or a private facility. Poverty and illogicality are important banes of medicine. Inadvertently, the doctors often become the target of people's anger. An increase in the number of malpractice suits has resulted in a costly and defensive medical practice. Worst of all is an increase in violence against doctors. The sacred tradition of doctor-patient relationship has been eroded and is severely threatened.

Meanwhile, I have entered a new phase of my professional career after completion of my years of service and started a new venture to continue with my work. Perhaps now, I can spare a little more time to go into the problems and persona of patients. I find the same personalities hidden in patients now as I had met few years, or a few decades earlier. I realize that people do not change, but the problems change. I am sure that we shall find newer solutions for our problems and dilemmas.

While driving back from the campus on the day of my superannuation from service in April 2014, I thought that based on averages, I must have seen over a hundred thousand patients at the Institute. But it seemed I have yet to learn the modern skills. I looked back and waved at my colleagues with whom I had the privilege of working over these years, and a large bunch of department alumni who had gathered to bid me farewell. I had the satisfaction that there exists a whole new generation to look into the complex issues. True to the words of Tennyson:

> 'The old order changeth, yielding place to new.
> And God fulfils himself in many ways,
> Lest one good custom should corrupt the world.'

GLOSSARY

A a

Allergic aspergillosis	An allergic problem which occurs in patients with asthma, due to sensitization with fungus aspergillus, colonized in the lungs.
Analgesic	A drug for relief of pain
Ashram	A Hindu religious retreat for worship, spiritual learning, music or yoga etc.

B b

BPL	Below Poverty Line
Ber	A Indian fruit, a kind of berry
Bhagiratha	An ancient king in Hindu mythology who brought the river Ganges on earth from the heavens
Bhagwan	Hindi word for God
Burfi	An Indian confectionary sweet made from condensed milk, sugar and other ingredients

C c

Cataract	Opacification of eye-lens causing poor vision which usually occurs in late middle age
Cesarian section	A surgical operation to deliver the fetus through an abdominal incision
Chandi	Hindu goddess; represents power- a destroyer of demons. Also known as Durga
Chatwaala	One who sells savoury snacks usually from a road- side stall or a food-cart
Chaulmoogra oil	Oil from seeds of chaulmoogra tree traditionally used in India and China for treatment of leprosy
Chhutta	A type of home-made cigar which is smoked with the burning end kept inside mouth- a reverse form of smoking; commonly in Eastern coast states of India
Chooda	A set of bangles of different colours (red, maroon and white) worn by a newly wed bride
Chyle	Milky white body fluid secreted by lymphatic glands
Chylothorax	Presence of abnormal chyle (milky fluid) in the pleural cavity
Cyanosis	Bluish hue of skin, tongue and other mucus membranes due to the deficiency of oxygen

D d

Dasehra	Hindu festival annually held to celebrate victory of Lord Rama over the demon king, Ravana.
Dhabha	A roadside eating joint serving local foods in India
Dhadhia	A person who weighs cereals on a balance in a cereal-market
Diwali	Hindu festival of lights widely celebrated all over India. The festival represents the return of lord Rama to his kingdom Ayodhya after defeating Ravana, the demon king
Dupatta	A kind of cotton or silk stole or scarf commonly worn by Indian women as part of their dress.
Durga	Hindu goddess of power, also known as Chandi.

E e

ECFMG	Educational Council for Foreign Medical Graduate- qualifying examination for foreign medical graduates to enter USA in the 1970s.
Ectopic beats	Heart beats due to disturbance of cardiac rhythm
Eid	Muslim religious festival celebrated worldwide that marks the end of a month of fasting

Episiotomy	An incision made in the perineum during child birth
Erythema ab igne	Skin redness and rash due to chronic exposure to heat; also known as hot water bottle rash or fire stains
Erythrocyte Sedimentation Rate	A medical test. High ESR commonly points to the presence of an active infection or inflammation
Extra-pyramidal symptoms	Abnormal involuntary movements and other symptoms mediated by neurological tracts which do not take origin from pyramids- the motor cortex in brain

F f

Fiberoptic bronchoscopy	Endoscopic procedure to examine the bronchial tree from inside with the help of a flexible fiberoptic instrument

G g

Ganesha	The widely worshipped Hindu god with elephant head, also known as Ganapati or Vinayaka
Gaumukh	Himalayan glacier at Gangotri which constitutes as the main source of the origin of river Ganges. Literally it means 'mouth of a cow'.

Gullain Barre Syndrome	Weakness of muscles of limbs, abdomen, chest and face developing rapidly usually within hours to days. Involvement of respiratory muscle poses threat to life.

H h

Havana	A Hindu ritual to make offerings to different gods around a consecrated fire.
Hemorrhage	Bleeding

J j

Jat Sikh	A sub-group of Sikhs in Punjab mostly engaged in farming

K k

Kangri	An earthen pot containing hot ambers used inside the clothes to keep warm- a common practice in Kashmir
Kapila	An ancient sage of *vedic* age with enormous spiritual powers
Karva chauth	A day of fast observed by married Hindu women for welfare and long lives of their husbands
Kos	An ancient Indian measurement unit for distance

| *Kumaris* | Traditionally in Nepal, an unmarried Hindu girl is designated a living goddess and worshipped by followers |
| *Kundli* | A horoscope prepared usually at birth to predict the future happenings |

L l

| *Lakshmana* | Younger brother of Lord Rama who had accompanied him in the exile |
| Leukoplakia | White patches or plaques inside the mouth. Leukoplakia may sometimes progress to a cancerous stage. |

M m

| *Mahabharata* | An ancient Hindu epic depicting the story of war fought in Kurukshetra between Pandavas and Kauravas |
| Mantoux test | Skin test employed in the diagnosis of tuberculosis |

N n

| *Nawab* | Title for the ruler of a state/ province within the Indian empire during the Mughal rule. |
| *Neem* | A tree of mahogany family native to India |

O o

Otorhinolaryngology	Medical specialty dealing with diseases of ear, nose and throat
Ozha	A traditional healer in India who practises alternative quack treatments

P p

Panchayat	A local self-government body for a village or a small town headed by a *Sarpanch*
Pandavas	The five sons of king Pandu (Yudhisthira, Bhima, Arjuna, Nakula and Sahadeva) who fought the Mahabharata war with Lord Krishna on their side
Pandit	A scholar or a teacher; also used for a priest expert in religious affairs
PET scan	Nuclear scanning with radioactive glucose FDG tracer used to detect cancers or other inflammatory conditions
Pickwickian Syndrome	A condition characterized by marked obesity and somnolence
Placenta	An organ that connects the developing fetus to the uterine wall during pregnancy. Placenta is expelled out during child-birth.

Pleural cavity	Potential space between the two layers of membranes (pleurae) surrounding the lungs
Pooja	Worship
Prasad	Religious offering to a deity, also distributed amongst followers.
Primigravida	A woman pregnant for the first time
Prostate	A gland in men which helps semen formation. It is present around the urethra (urinary tube) between the urinary bladder and the penis. Prostate is present just in front of rectum, therefore palpated through per-rectal examination
Pulmonology	Medical specialty dealing with diseases of lungs and respiratory system

Q q

Qanungo	Designation for a government revenue official dealing with landed property.

R r

Rama	One of the most important Hindu deity who as the 7ᵗʰ incarnation of Lord Vishnu, lived as the King of Ayodhya

Ravana	The demon king of Lanka in the Hindu epic Ramayana who was finally defeated by Lord Rama
*Rehri*market	A kind of flea market in India
Ripening of cervix	An impending sign of labour when cervix becomes soft and distensible to facilitate delivery

S s

Sahibzada	Son of an honourable person. The term is specifically used for the four sons of Shri Guru Gobind Singh Ji, the 10th Sikh Guru. Two of the four *sahibzadas* were bricked alive by the Nawab for their refusal to accept his dictat to change their religion
Sanjeevni booti	Divine herb which was used to bring Lakshman (Younger brother of Lord Rama) back to life when he lost consciousness in war
Sarcoidosis	A non-infectious disease which greatly mimics tuberculosis
Sarpanch	Elected head of a village level governing body.
Sepsis	Severe blood infection with micro-organisms
Sevian	Indian dessert of vermicelli
Sherwani	Long coat traditionally worn by Muslim aristocrats especially on a formal occasion

Stroke	Sudden paralysis or other body deficit resulting from block of or bleeding from an artery in the brain.
Stupa	A Budhist structure often with buried ashes of monks.
Susruta samhita	An ancient Sanskrit text of surgery known since about one millennia B.C.
Sutra sthana	First part of Charaka samhita, an ancient book on Ayurveda.

T t

Tantrik	A rustic sadhu who worship Goddess Durga or Lord Shiva, sometimes believed to perform acts of black magic.
Tehsildar	Revenue administrative officer senior to a *qanungo*.
Tetanus	An infection caused by bacteria Clostridium tetani; characterized by muscle spasms
Toap	A Hindi word for a cannon – a big gun. It is sometimes used to magnify the power of an individual
Tracheostomy	Surgical hole created in the trachea i.e. the wind pipe

V v

Ventilation	Respiration (i.e. the process of breathing in and out)
Ventilator	A mechanized, automated advanced pump used to infuse air and oxygen in the body to maintain functions of normal respiratory system

W w

Waheguru	Sikhs' reference to the supreme God. Literally it means 'Wonderful Teacher'.
Weaning	The process of systematically reducing and finally removing respiratory (ventilatory) assistance

Y y

Yama or Yamaraj	God of death in Hindu (Vedic) mythology
Yaksha	Broad category of mythical characters in ancient India
Yudhishtra	Eldest of five *Pandava* brothers who never spoke a lie

Printed in the United States
By Bookmasters